2 (If You're Wondering If I Want You To) I Want You To

12 I'm Your Daddy

18 The Girl Got Hot

25 Can't Stop Partying

31 Put Me Back Together

39 Trippin' Down the Freeway

46 Love Is the Answer

53 Let It All Hang Out

61 In the Mall

69 I Don't Want to Let You Go

78 GUITAR NOTATION LEGEND

Music transcriptions by Pete Billmann

ISBN 978-1-4234-7526-2

7777 W. BLUEMOUND RD. P.O. BOX 13819 MILWAUKEE, WI 53213

In Australia Contact:
Hal Leonard Australia Pty. Ltd.
4 Lentara Court
Cheltenham, Victoria, 3192 Australia
Email: ausadmin@halleonard.com.au

For all works contained herein:
Unauthorized copying, arranging, adapting, recording, Internet posting, public performance,
or other distribution of the printed music in this publication is an infringement of copyright.
Infringers are liable under the law.

Visit Hal Leonard Online at
www.halleonard.com

(If You're Wondering if I Want You To) I Want You To

Words and Music by Rivers Cuomo and Butch Walker

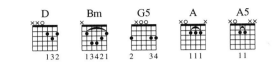

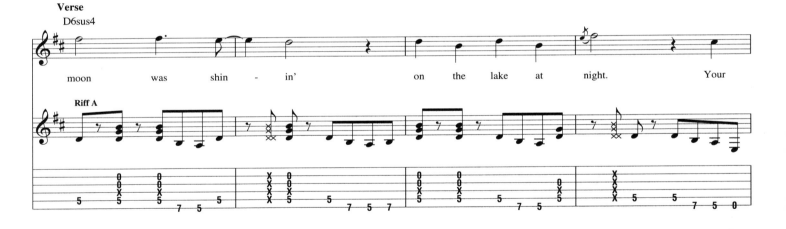

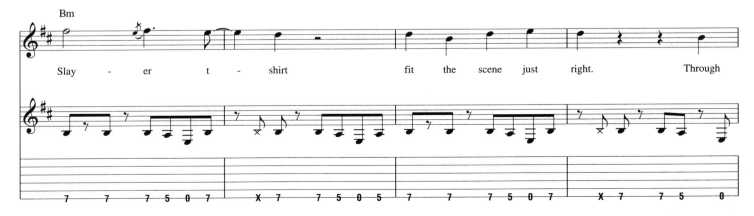

Copyright © 2009 E.O. Smith Music, EMI April Music Inc. and I Eat Publishing For Breakfast
All Rights for E.O. Smith Music Administered by Wixen Music Publishing, Inc.
All Rights for I Eat Publishing For Breakfast Controlled and Administered by EMI April Music Inc.
International Copyright Secured All Rights Reserved

*See top of first page of song for chord diagrams pertaining to rhythm slashes.
**Doubled throughout

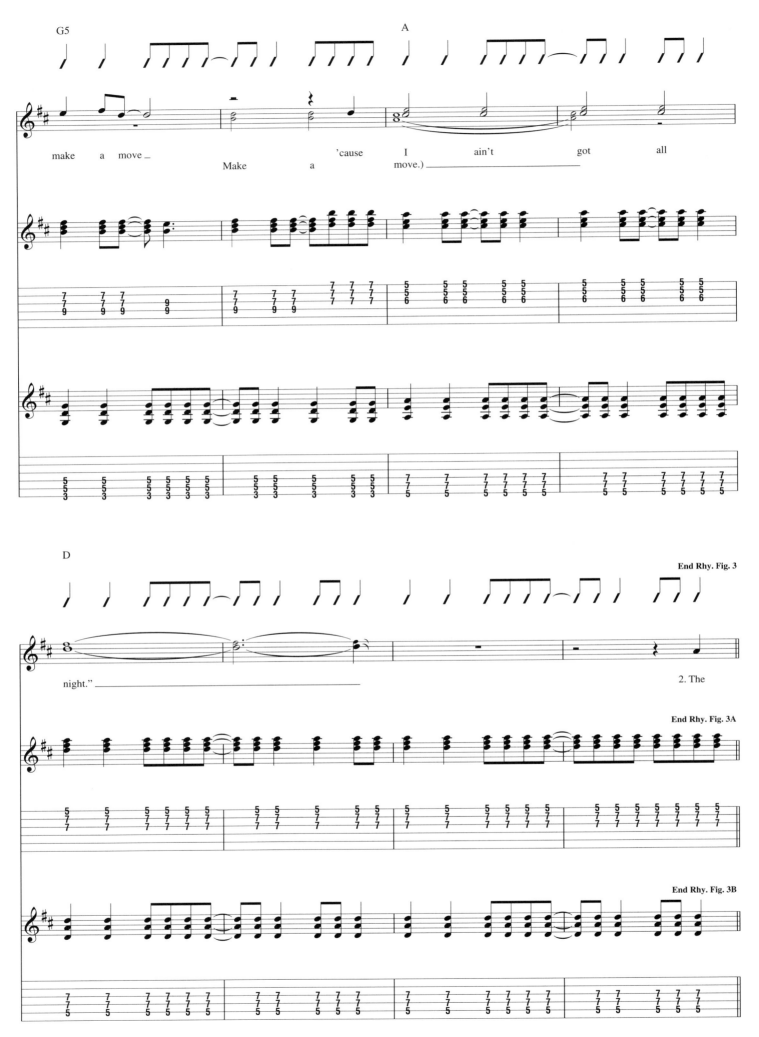

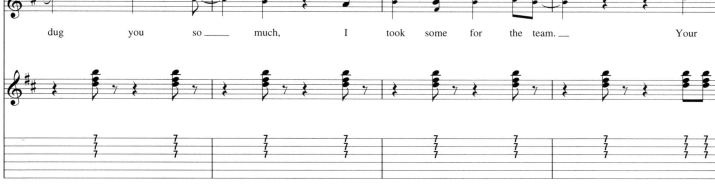

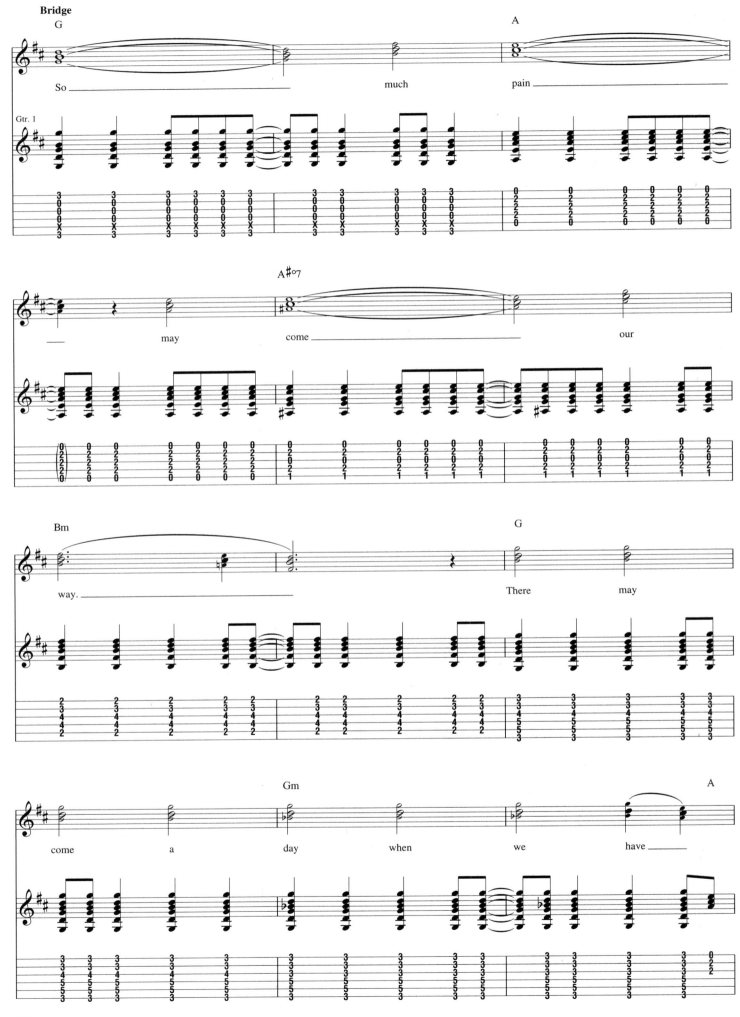

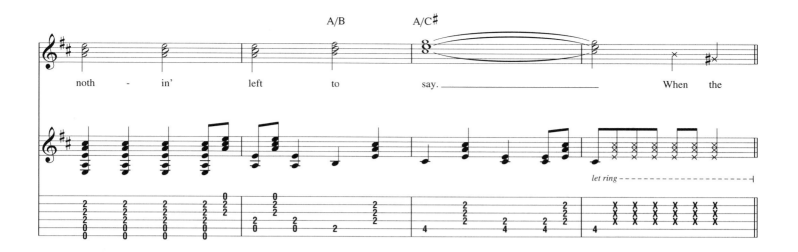

Pre-Chorus

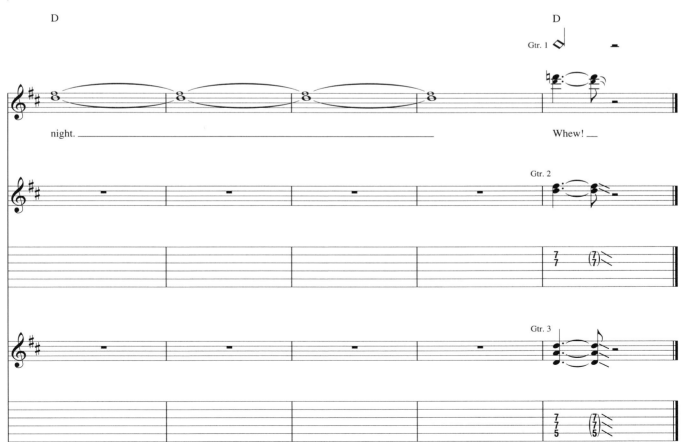

I'm Your Daddy

Words and Music by Rivers Cuomo and Lukasz Gottwald

Tune down 1/2 step:
(low to high) E♭-A♭-D♭-G♭-B♭-E♭

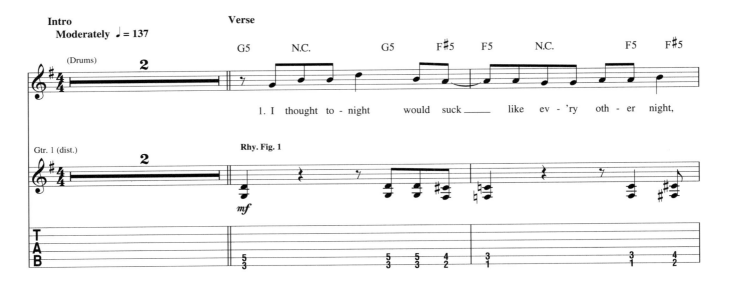

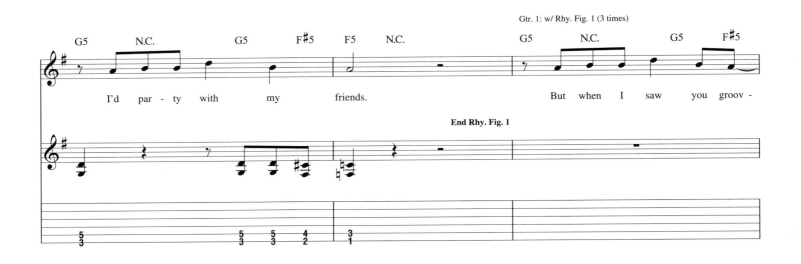

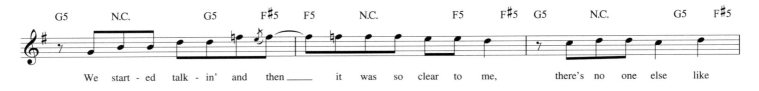

Copyright © 2009 E.O. Smith Music and Kasz Money Publishing
All Rights for E.O. Smith Music Administered by Wixen Music Publishing, Inc.
All Rights for Kasz Money Publishing Administered by Kobalt Music Publishing America, Inc.
International Copyright Secured All Rights Reserved

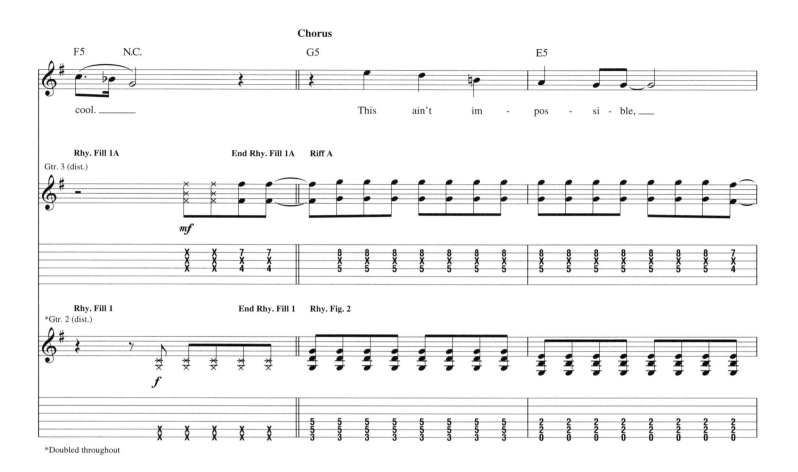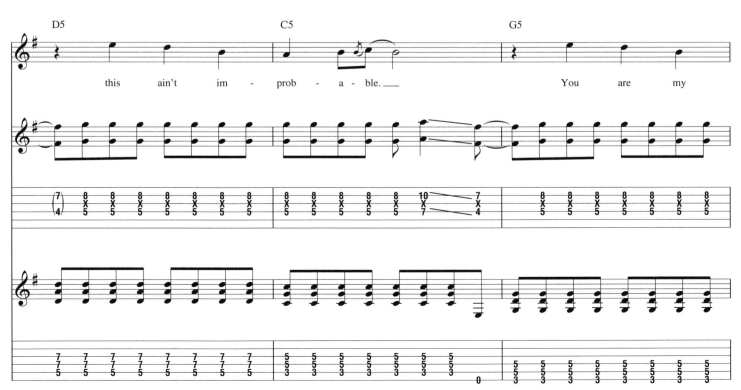

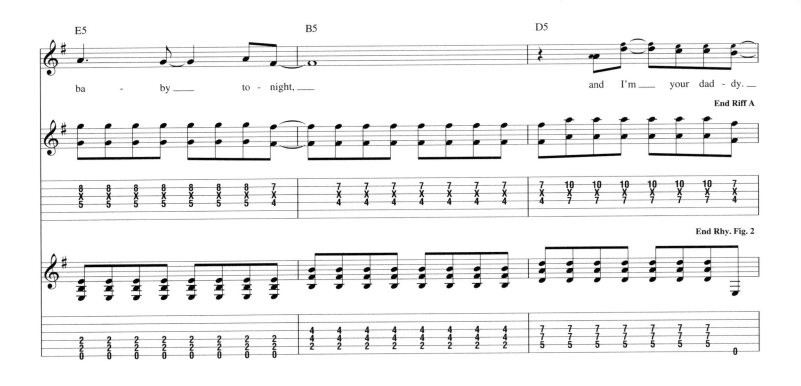
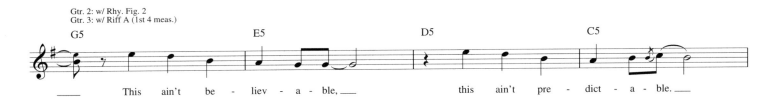
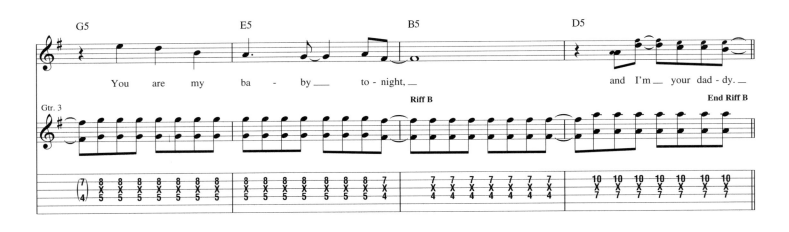

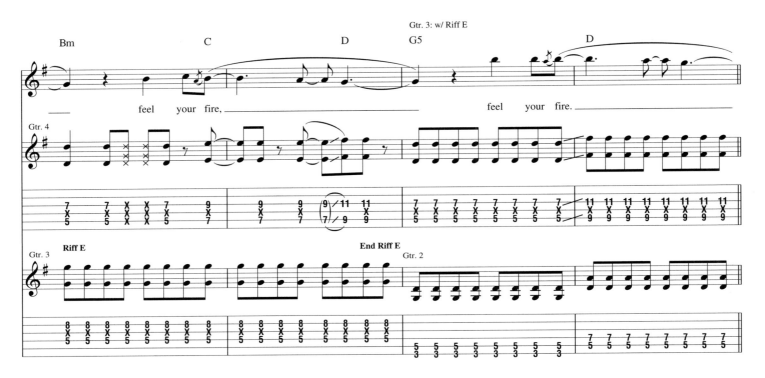
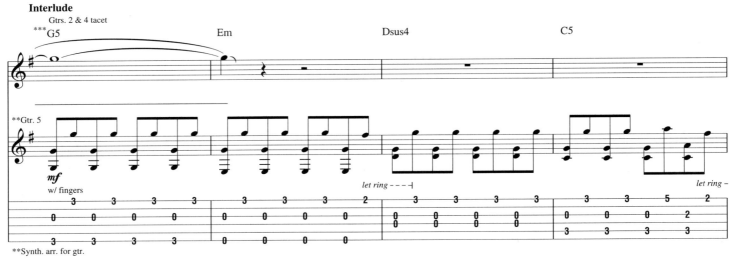

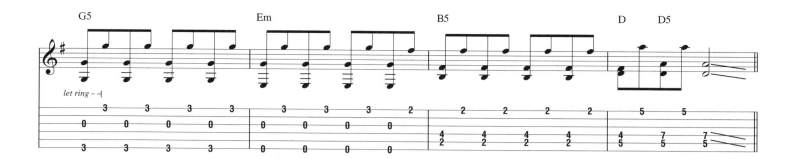
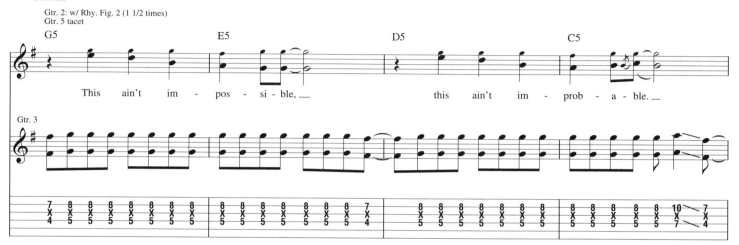
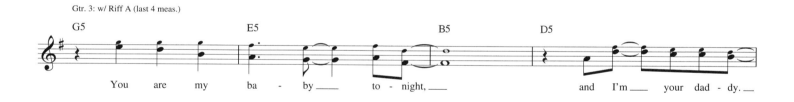
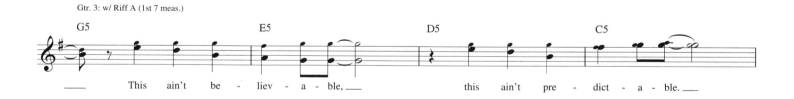
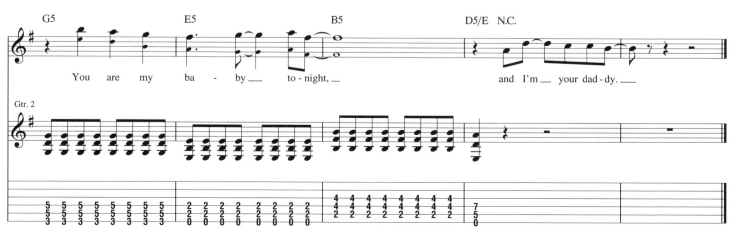

The Girl Got Hot

Words and Music by Rivers Cuomo and Butch Walker

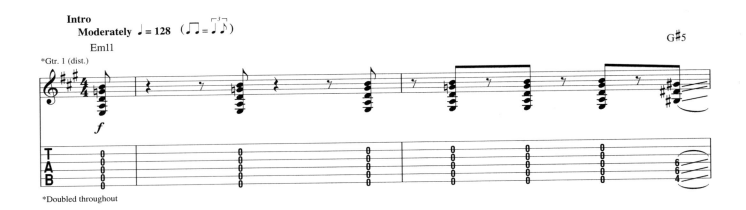
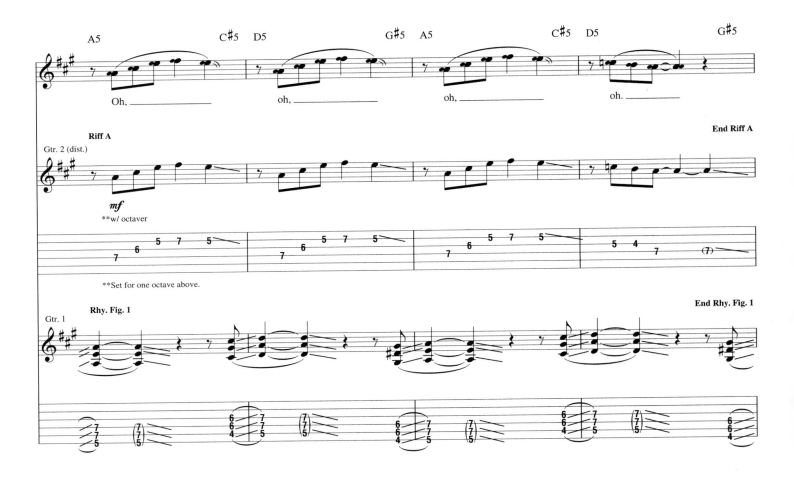

Copyright © 2009 E.O. Smith Music, EMI April Music Inc. and I Eat Publishing For Breakfast
All Rights for E.O. Smith Music Administered by Wixen Music Publishing, Inc.
All Rights for I Eat Publishing For Breakfast Controlled and Administered by EMI April Music Inc.
International Copyright Secured   All Rights Reserved

Verse

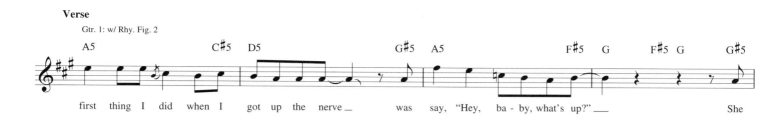

Pre-Chorus

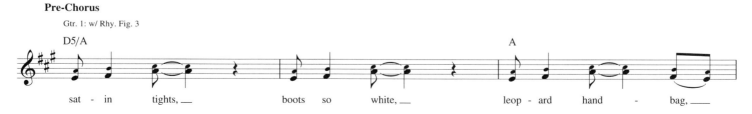

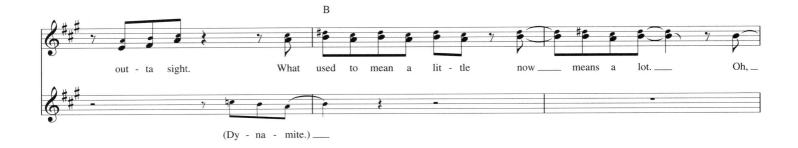
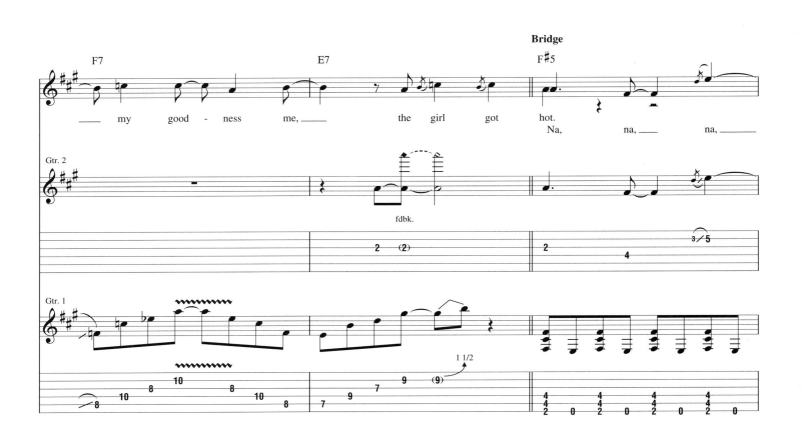

Pre-Chorus

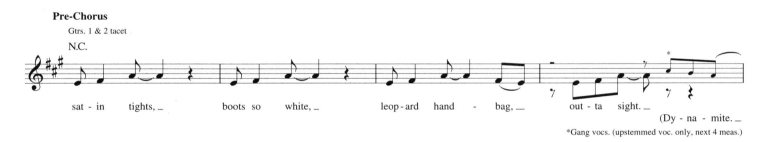

Chorus

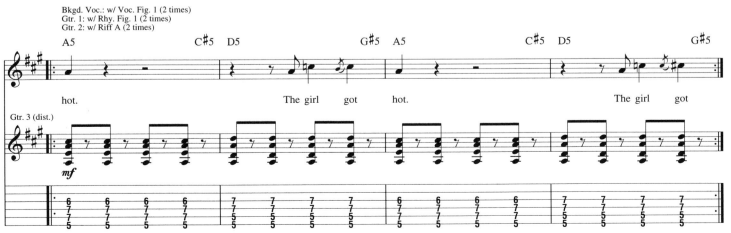

Outro-Chorus
Bkgd. Voc.: w/ Voc. Fig. 1 (2 times)
Gtr. 2: w/ Riff A (3 times)
Gtr. 3: w/ Riff B (4 times)

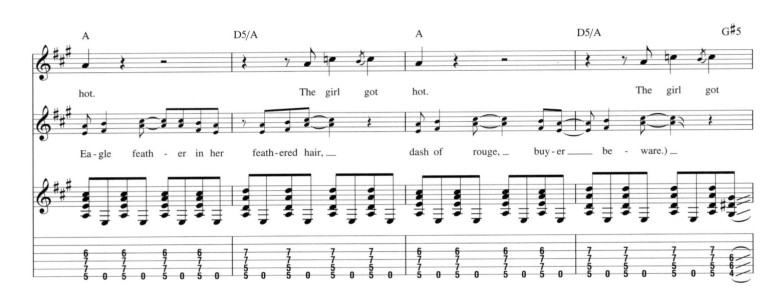

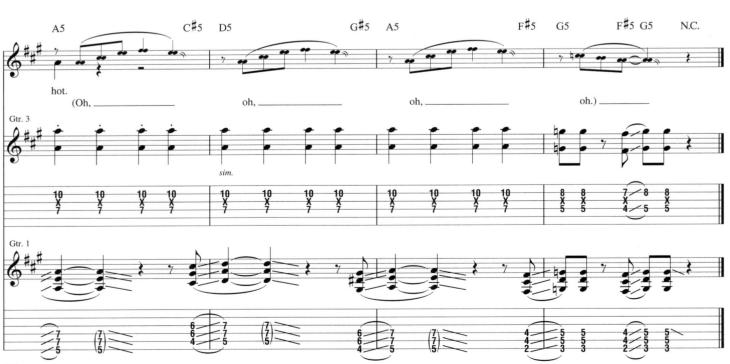

Can't Stop Partying

Words and Music by Rivers Cuomo, Jermaine Dupri, Jamal Jones and Dwayne Carter

Tune down 1/2 step:
(low to high) E♭-A♭-D♭-G♭-B♭-E♭

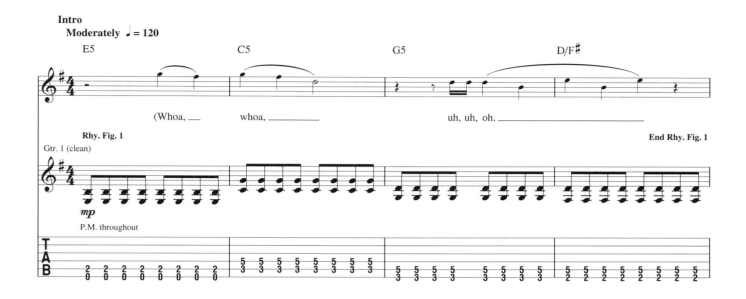

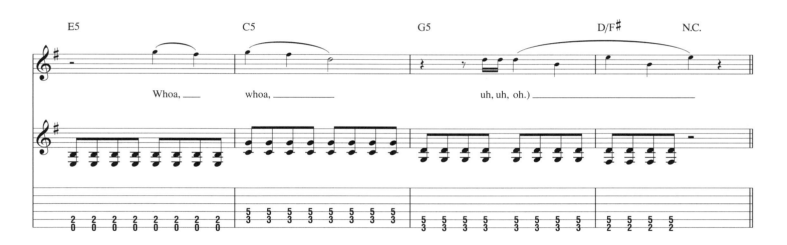

Copyright © 2008, 2009 E.O. Smith Music, EMI April Music Inc., Shaniah Cymone Music, Songs Of Universal, Inc.,
My Diet Starts Tomorrow, Inc., Warner-Tamerlane Publishing Corp. and Young Money Publishing Inc.
All Rights for E.O. Smith Music Administered by Wixen Music Publishing, Inc.
All Rights for Shaniah Cymone Music Controlled and Administered by EMI April Music Inc.
All Rights for My Diet Starts Tomorrow, Inc. Controlled and Administered by Songs Of Universal, Inc.
International Copyright Secured   All Rights Reserved

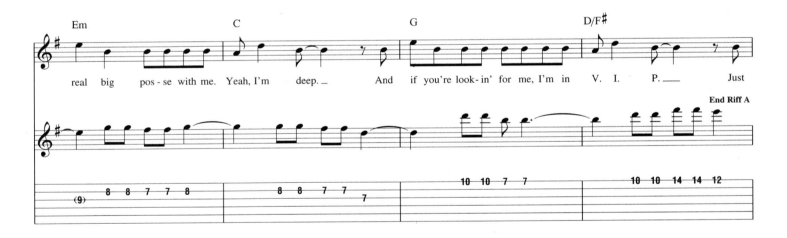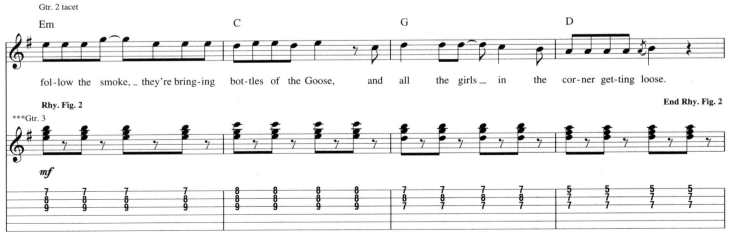

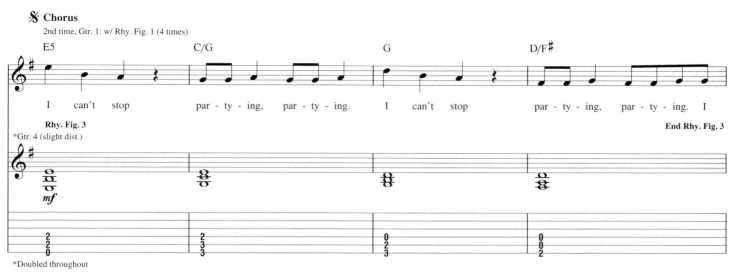

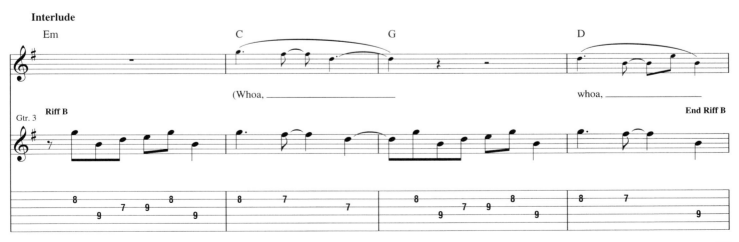

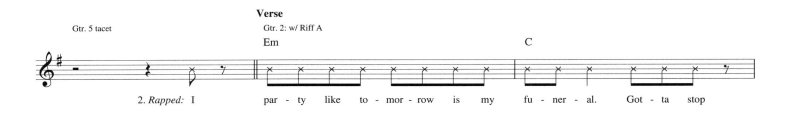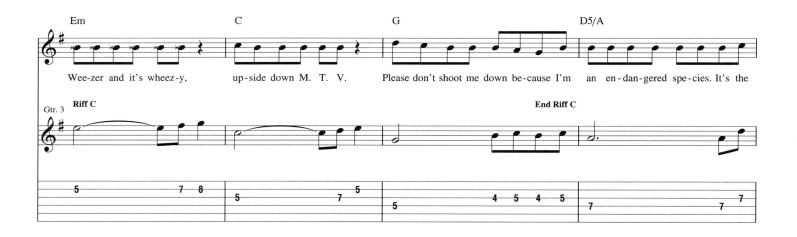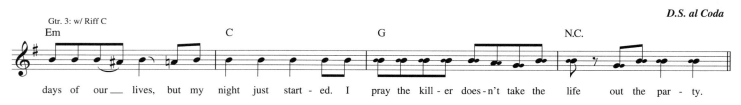

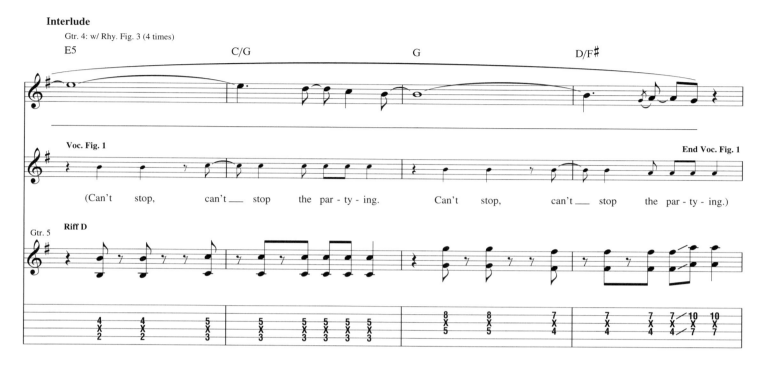
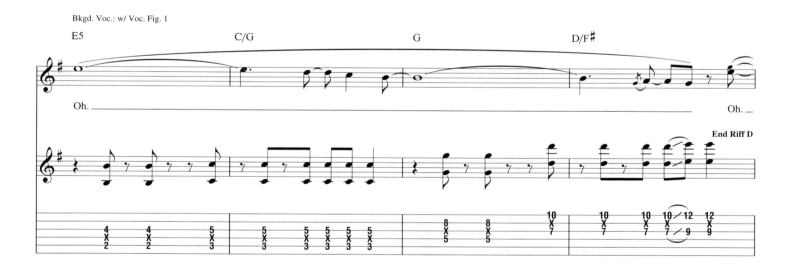
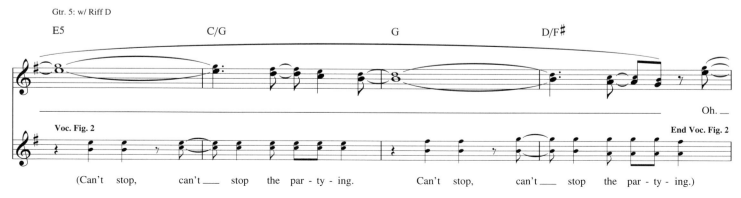

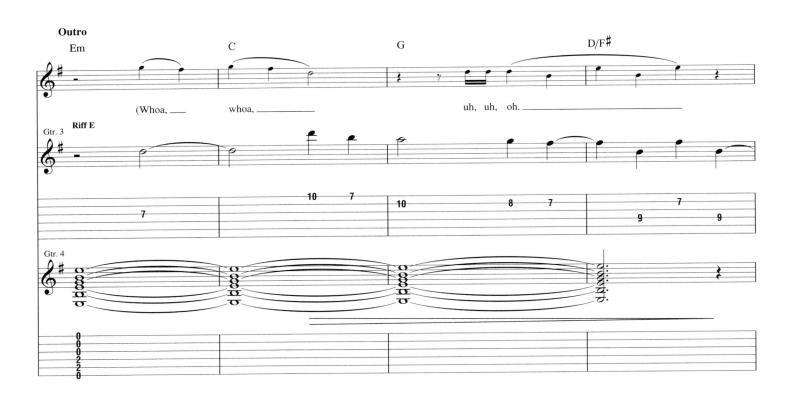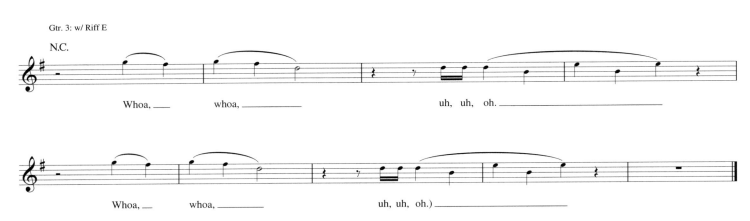

Put Me Back Together

Words and Music by Rivers Cuomo, Tyson Ritter and Nick Wheeler

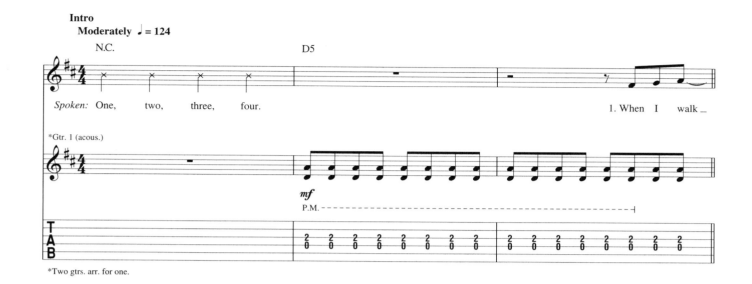

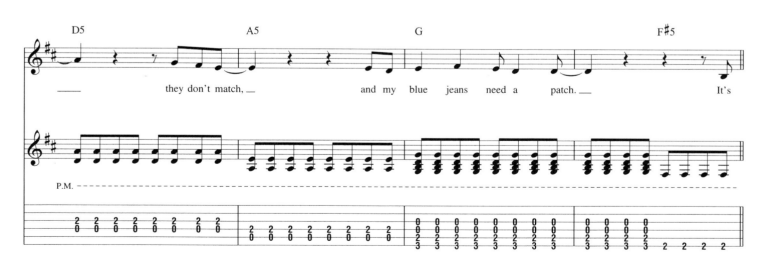

Copyright © 2009 E.O. Smith Music, Universal Music - MGB Songs and Smells Like Phys Ed Music
All Rights for E.O. Smith Music Administered by Wixen Music Publishing, Inc.
All Rights for Smells Like Phys Ed Music Administered by Universal Music - MGB Songs
International Copyright Secured   All Rights Reserved

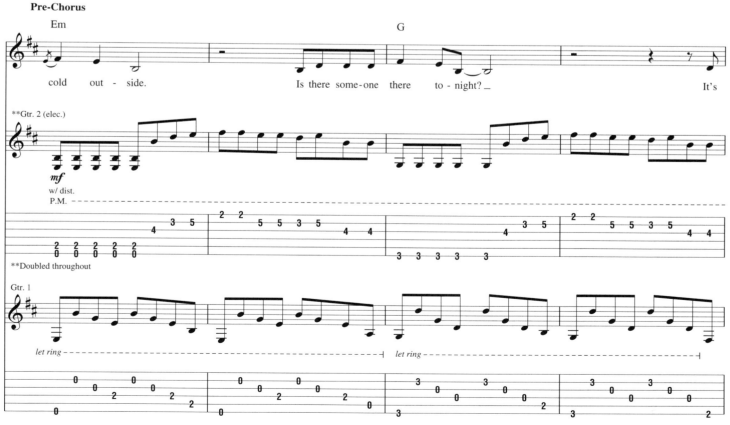

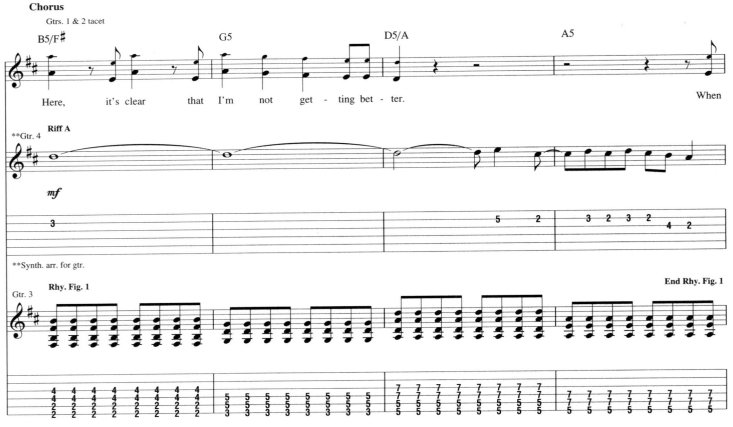

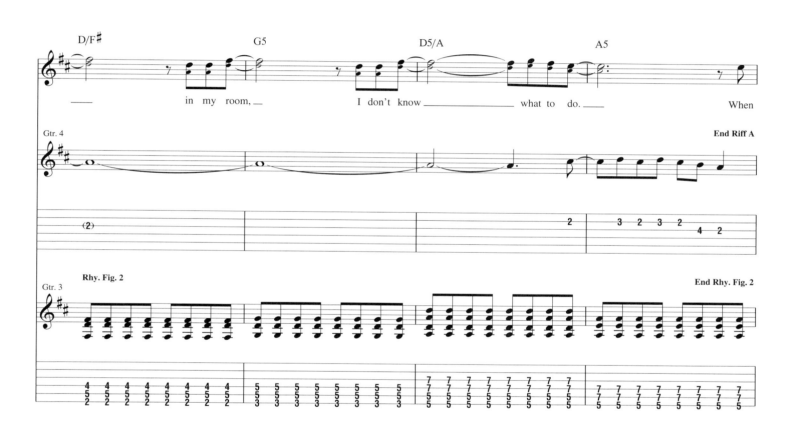

Bridge

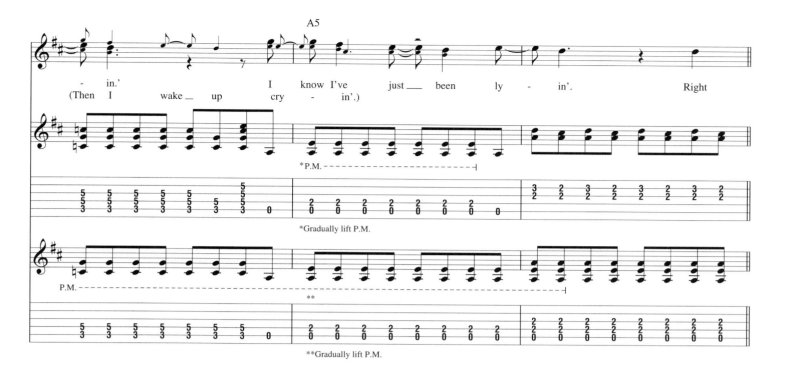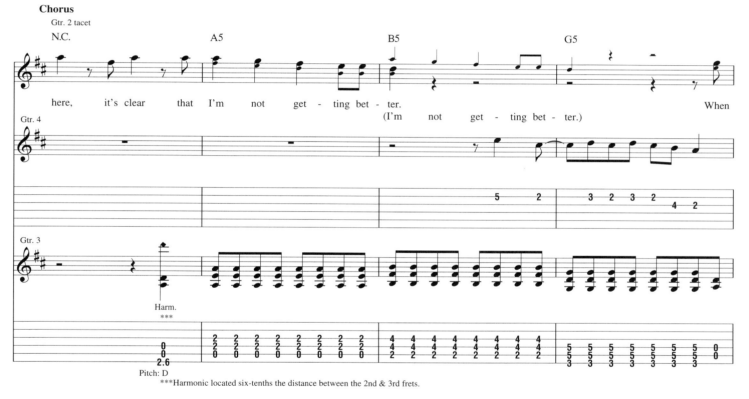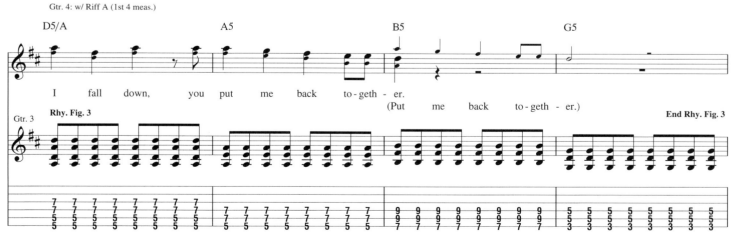

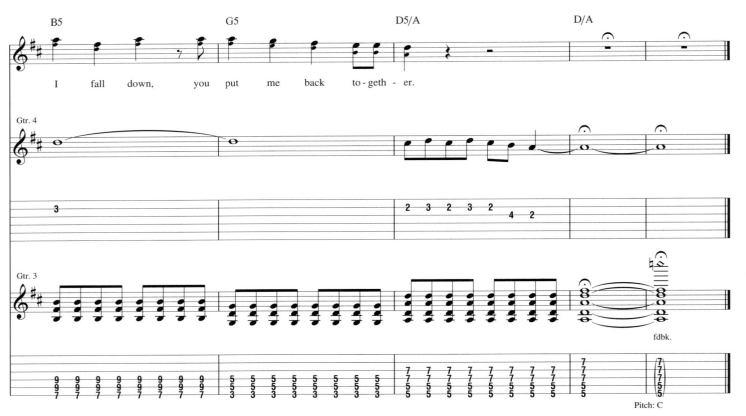

Trippin' Down the Freeway

Words and Music by Rivers Cuomo

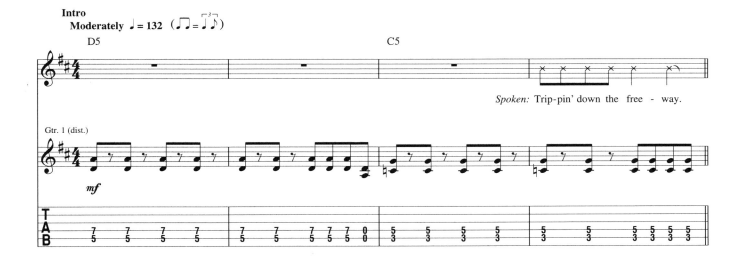

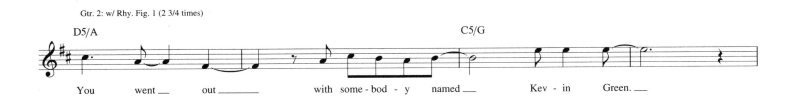

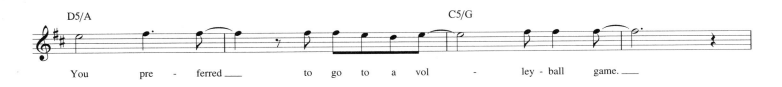

Copyright © 2009 E.O. Smith Music
All Rights Administered by Wixen Music Publishing, Inc.
International Copyright Secured   All Rights Reserved

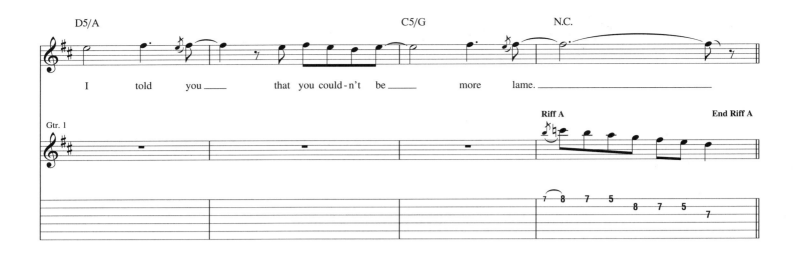
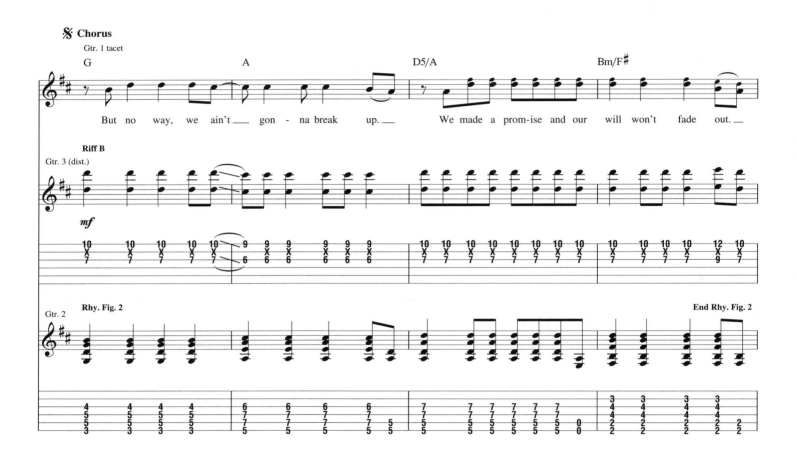
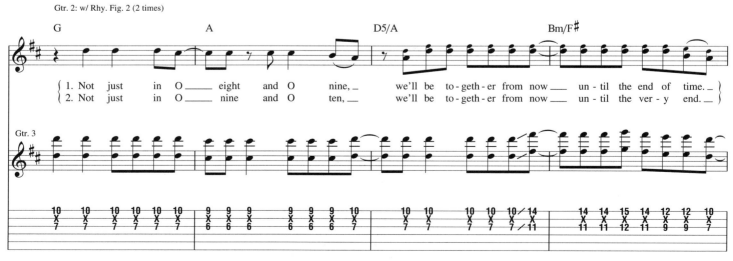

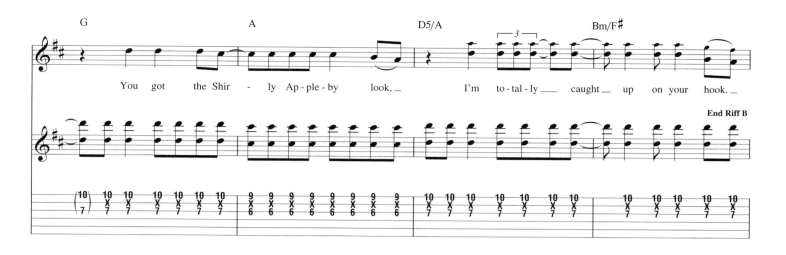
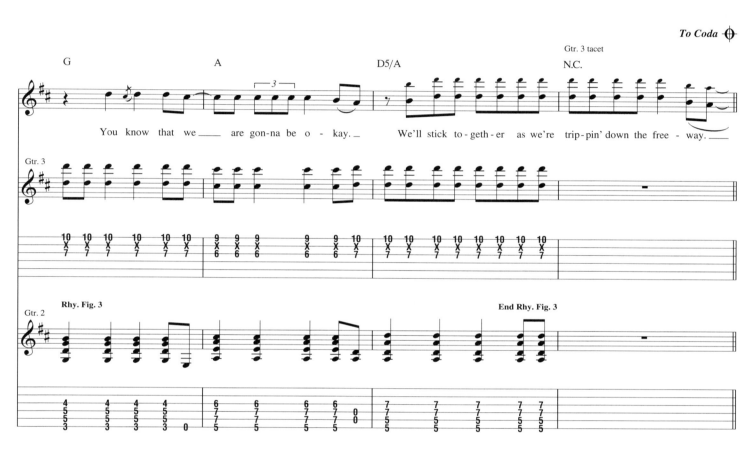

Interlude

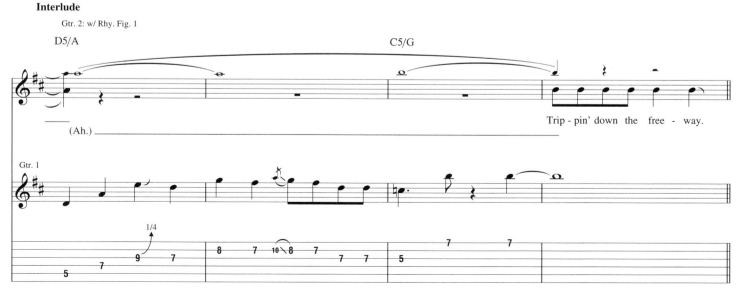

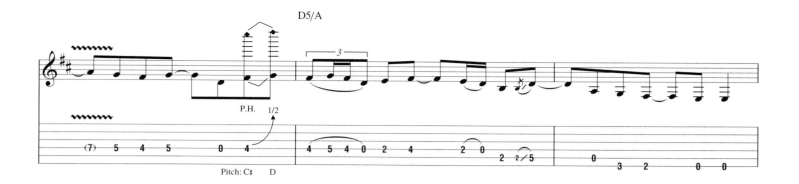

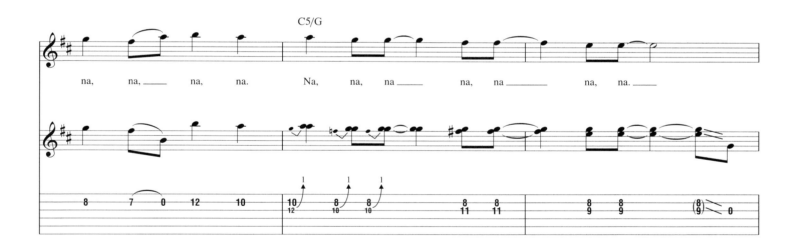
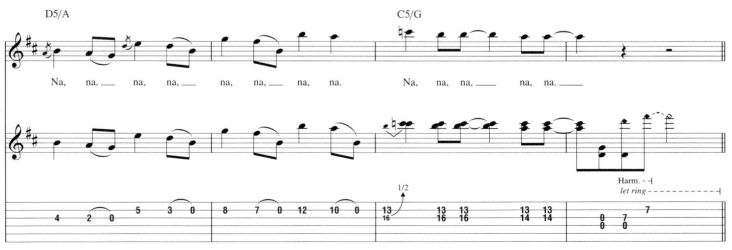

43

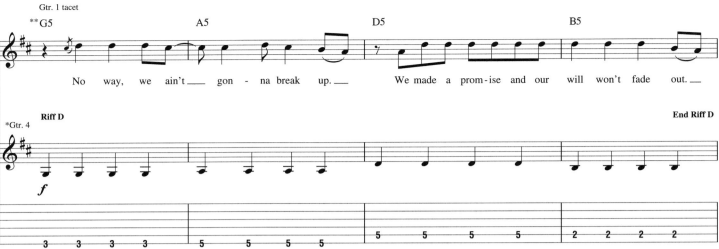

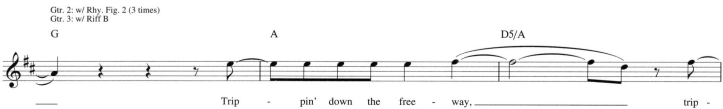

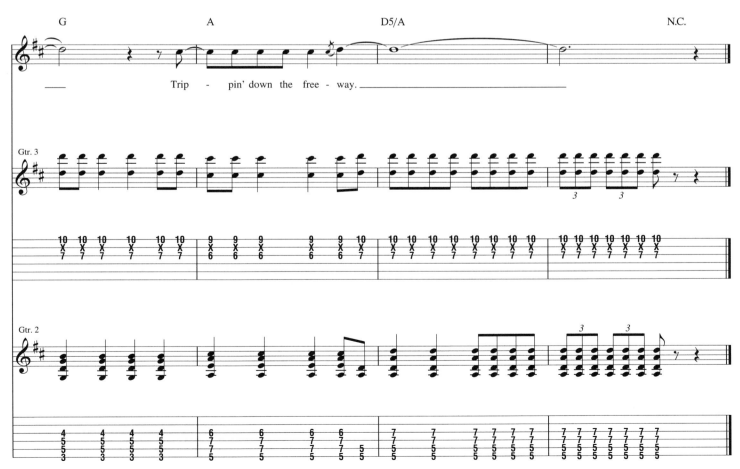

Love Is the Answer

Words and Music by Rivers Cuomo, Amrita Sen, Ananda Sen, Nishat Khan and Garret Lee

Gtrs. 3–8: Drop D tuning:
(low to high) D-A-D-G-B-E

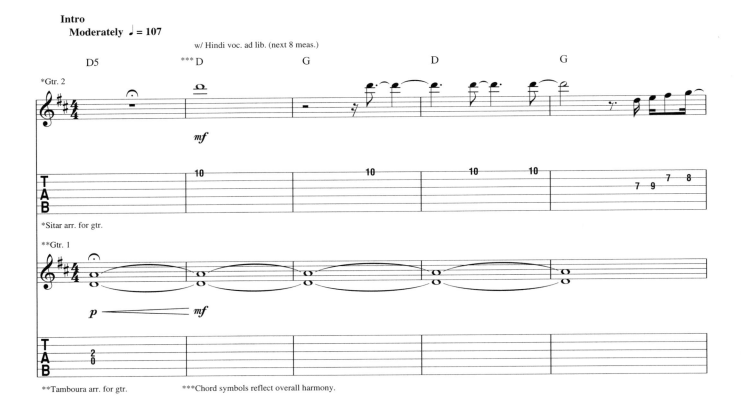

Copyright © 2009 E.O. Smith Music and Chrysalis Music Ltd.
All Rights for E.O. Smith Music Administered by Wixen Music Publishing, Inc.
All Rights for Chrysalis Music Ltd. in the U.S. and Canada Administered by Chrysalis Music
International Copyright Secured   All Rights Reserved

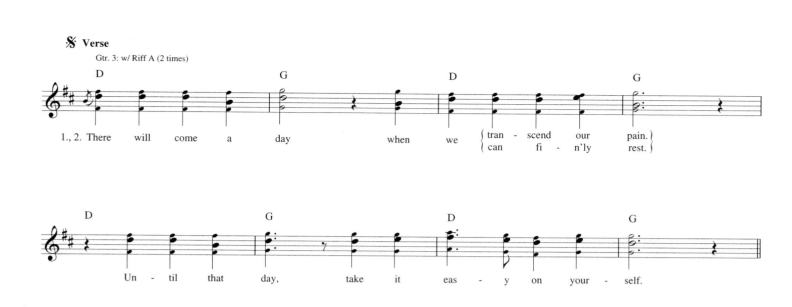

47

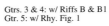

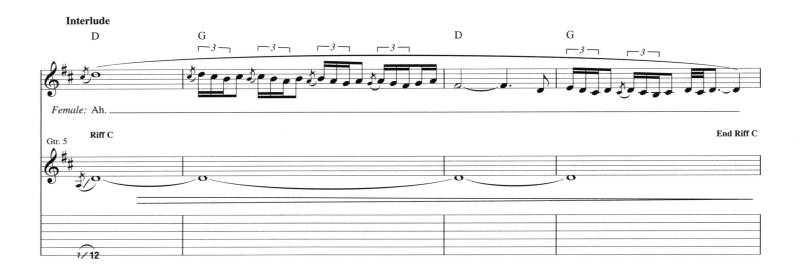

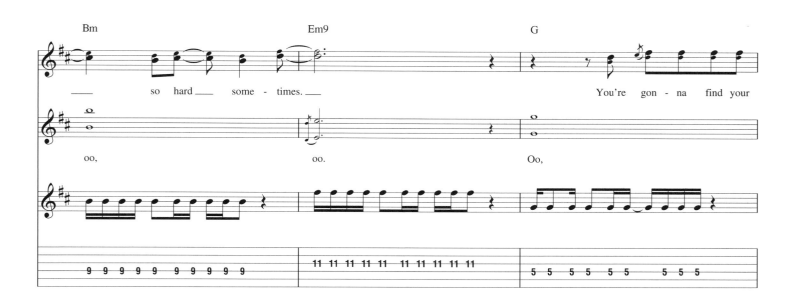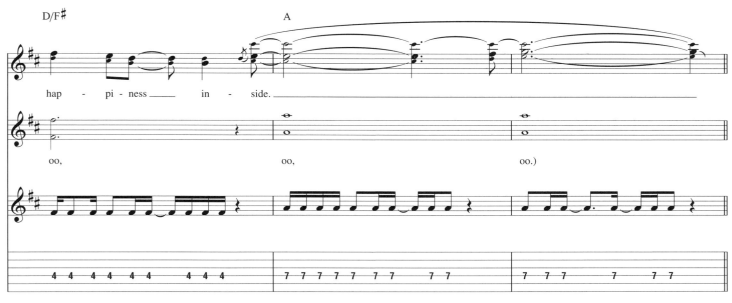

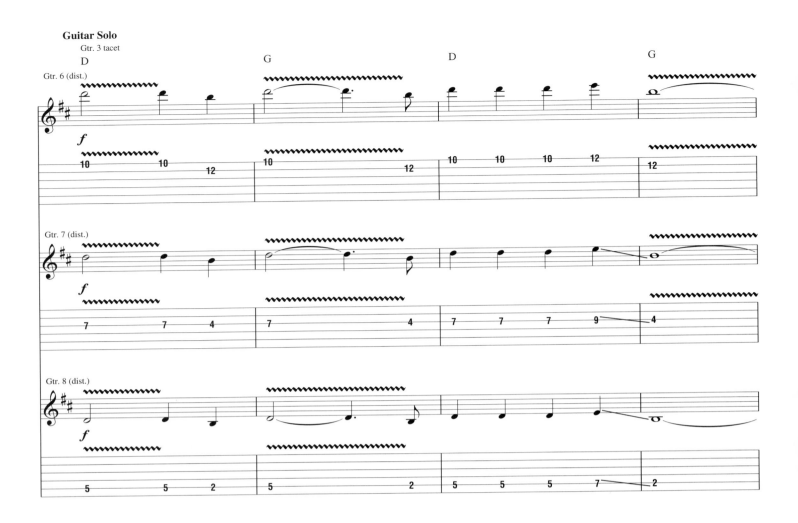

Interlude

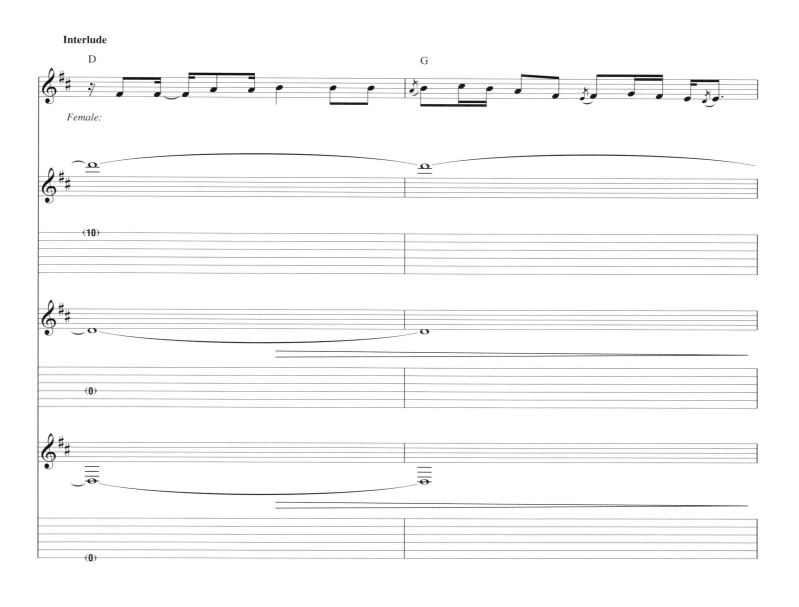

Female:

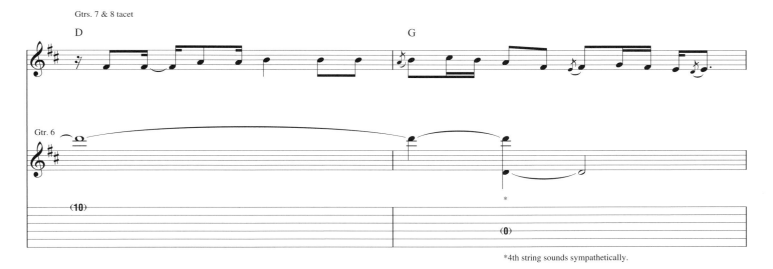

*4th string sounds sympathetically.

Gtr. 6 tacet

w/ male Hindi voc. (next 3 meas.)

51

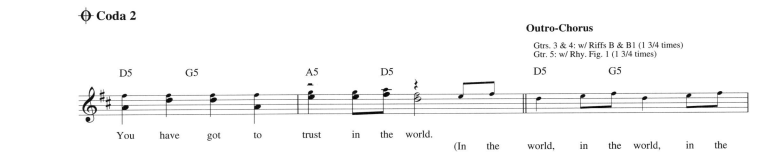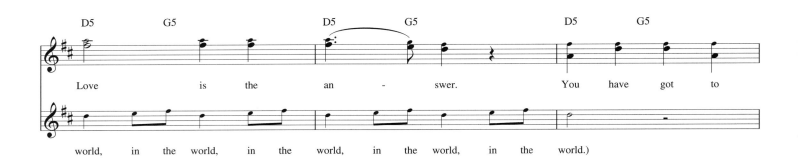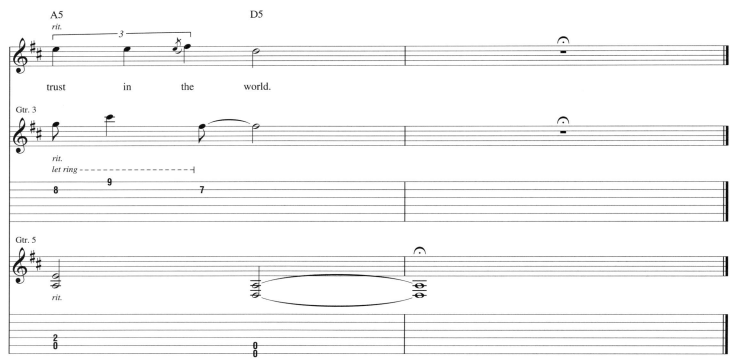

Let It All Hang Out

Words and Music by Rivers Cuomo, Jermaine Dupri and Garret Lee

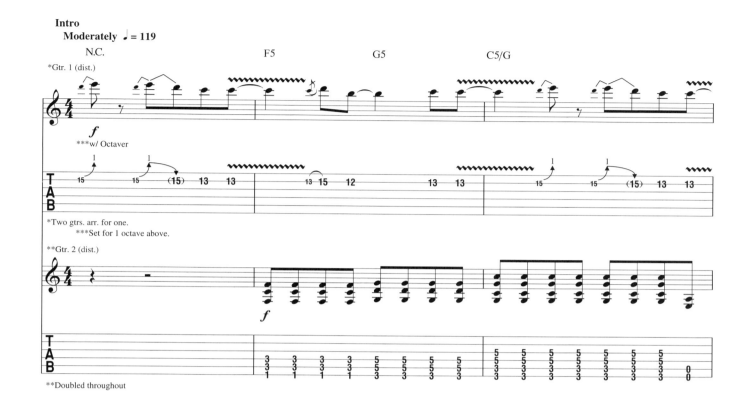

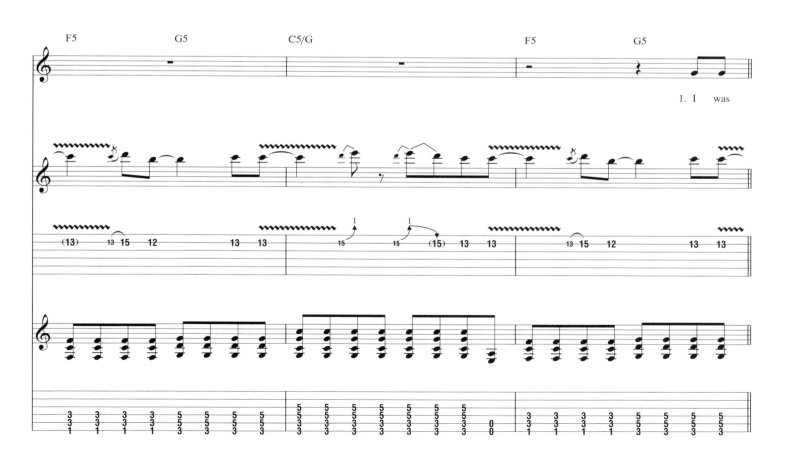

Copyright © 2009 E.O. Smith Music, EMI April Music Inc., Shaniah Cymone Music and Chrysalis Music Ltd.
All Rights for E.O. Smith Music Administered by Wixen Music Publishing, Inc.
All Rights for Shaniah Cymone Music Controlled and Administered by EMI April Music Inc.
All Rights for Chrysalis Music Ltd. in the U.S. and Canada Administered by Chrysalis Music
International Copyright Secured   All Rights Reserved

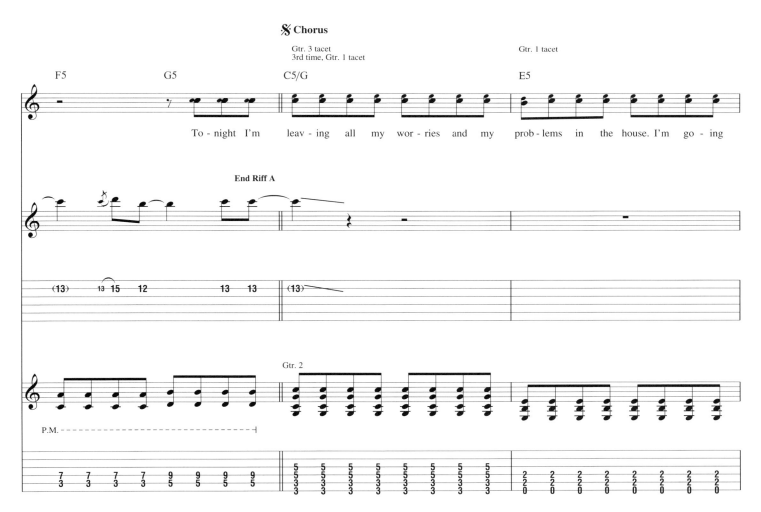

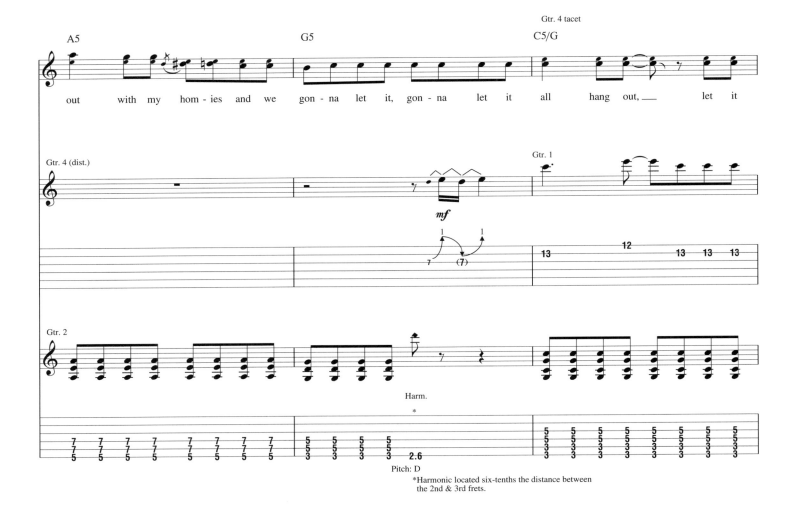
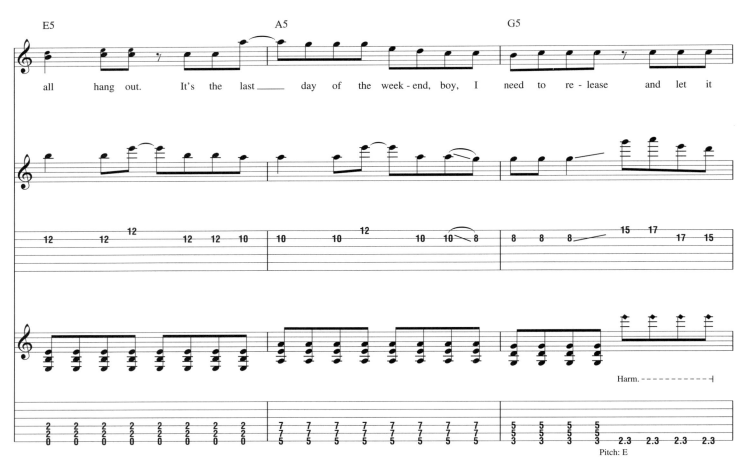

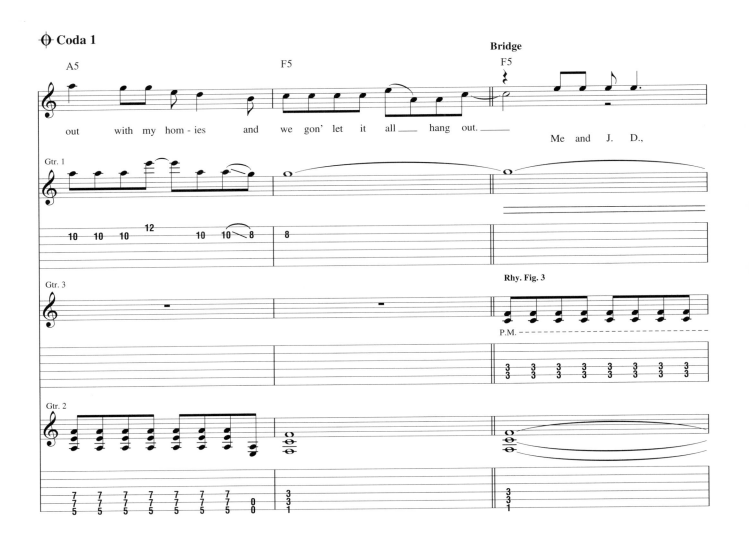
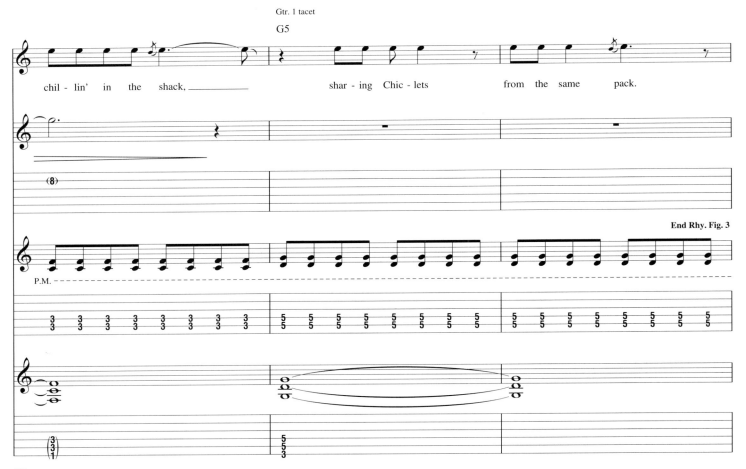

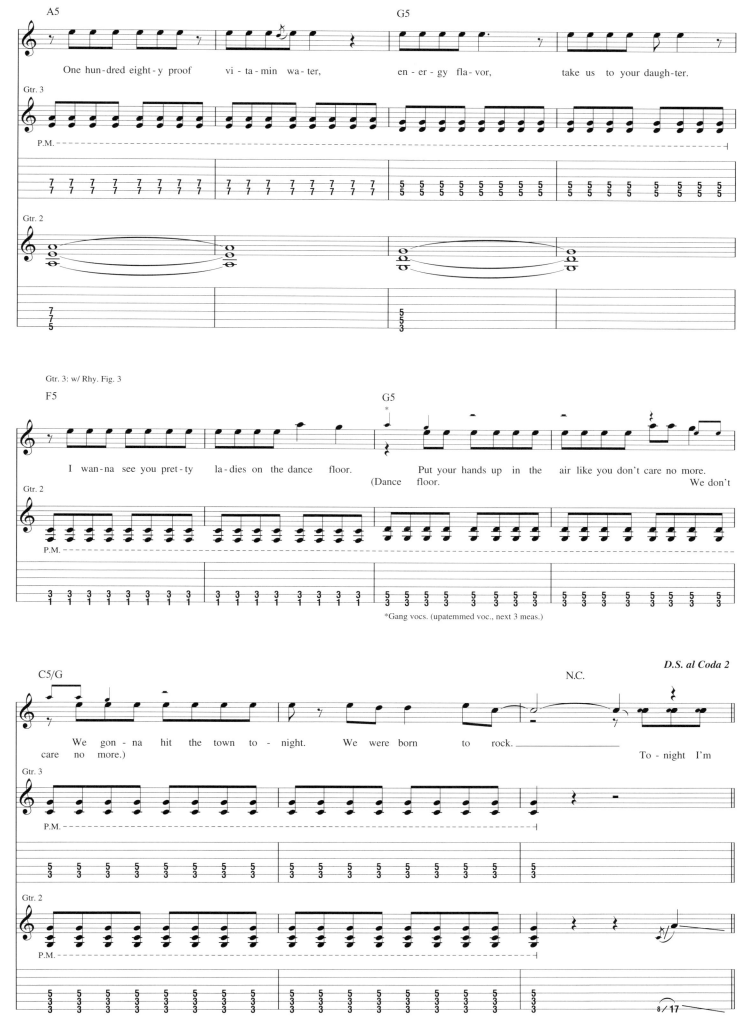

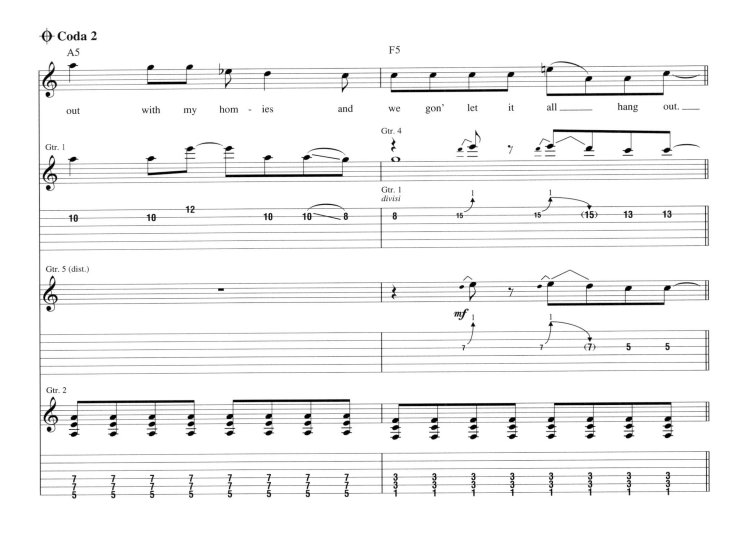

In the Mall

Words and Music by Patrick Wilson

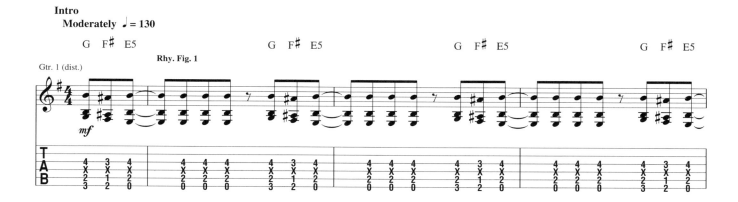

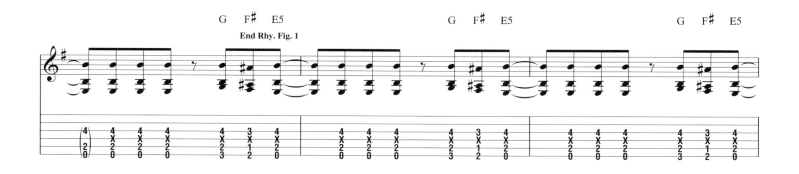

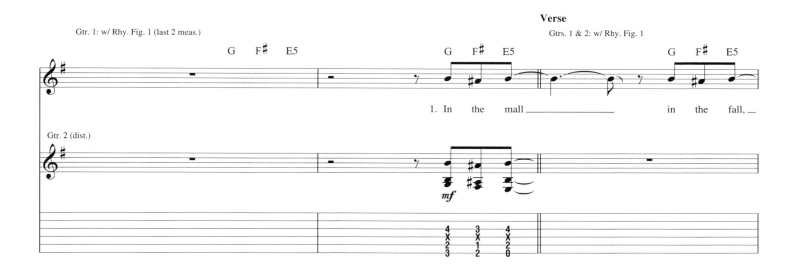

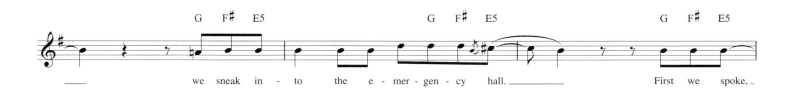

Copyright © 2009 Fie!
All Rights Administered by Wixen Music Publishing, Inc.
International Copyright Secured   All Rights Reserved

Verse

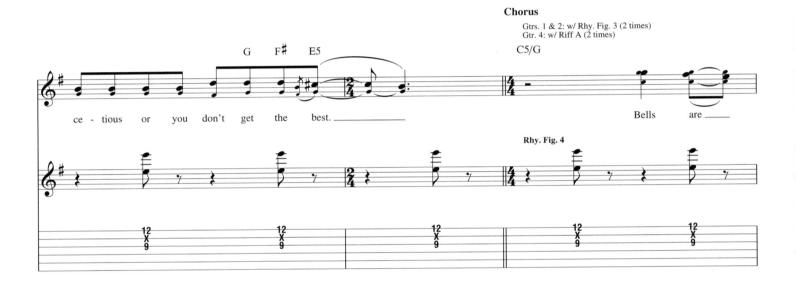

Bridge

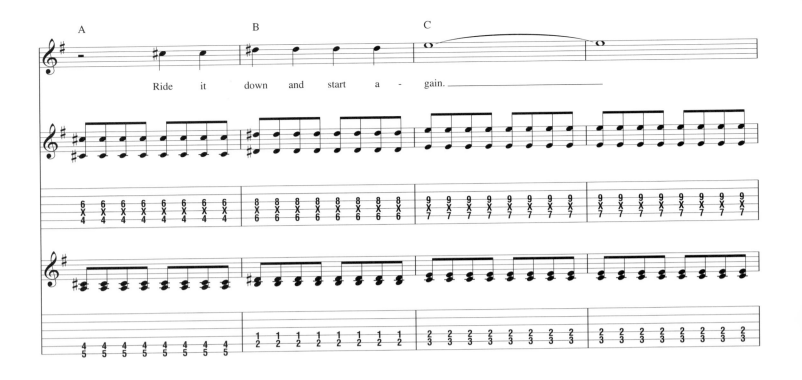
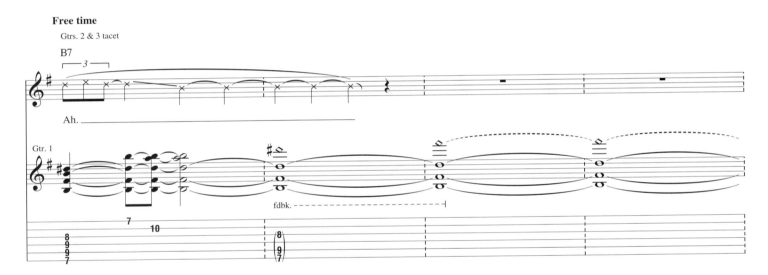
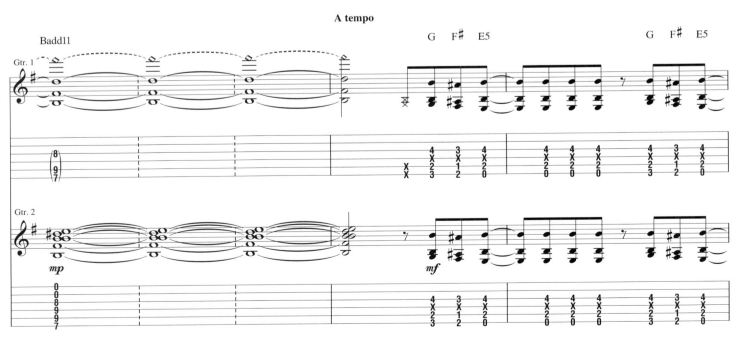

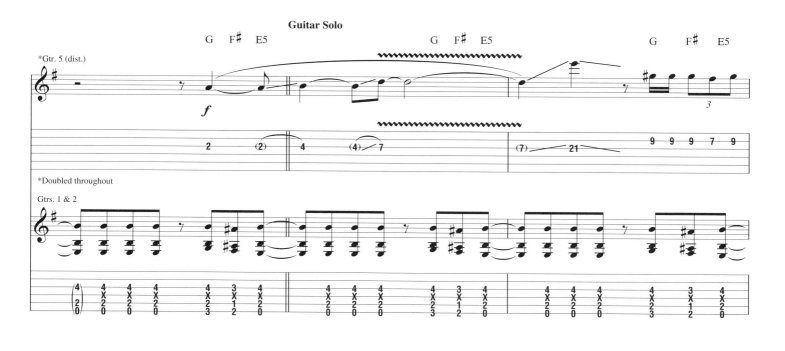
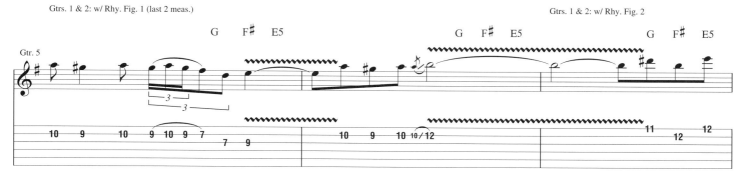
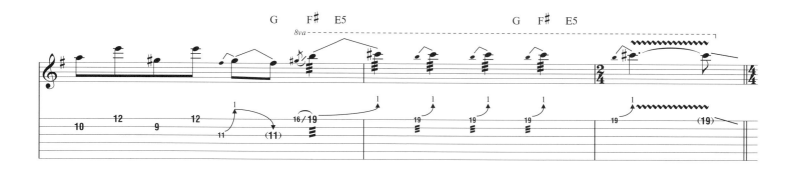
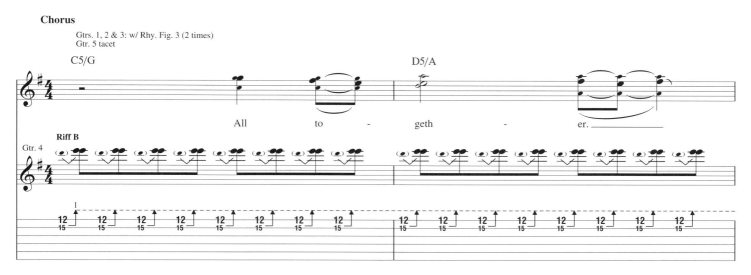

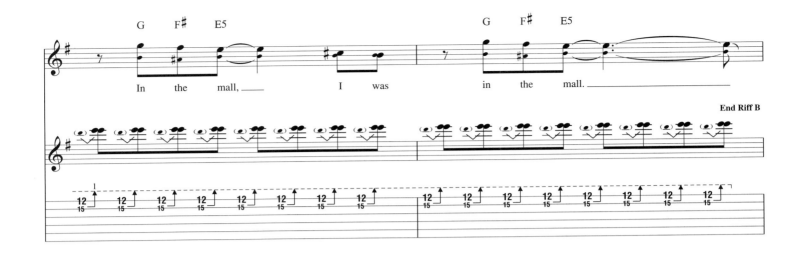

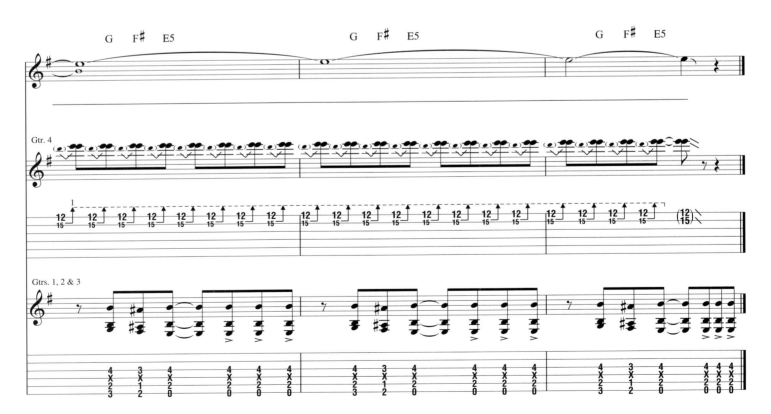

I Don't Want to Let You Go

Words and Music by Rivers Cuomo

Tune down 1/2 step:
(low to high) E♭-A♭-D♭-G♭-B♭-E♭

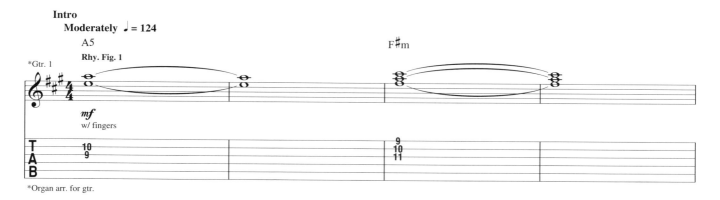

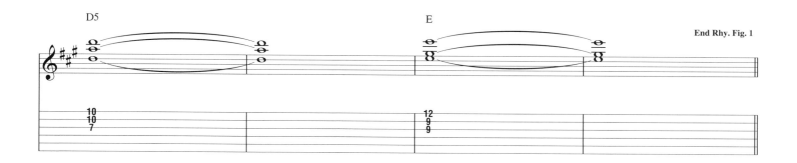

Verse

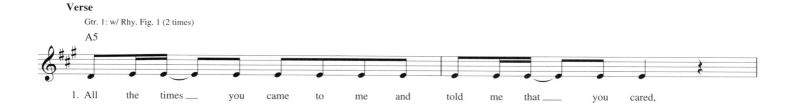

1. All the times you came to me and told me that you cared,

I was dream-in' of hap-py days that we both could share. May-be I got too ex-cit-ed and

may-be you freaked out. May-be I just have to call you up and scream and shout.

Copyright © 2009 E.O. Smith Music
All Rights Administered by Wixen Music Publishing, Inc.
International Copyright Secured   All Rights Reserved

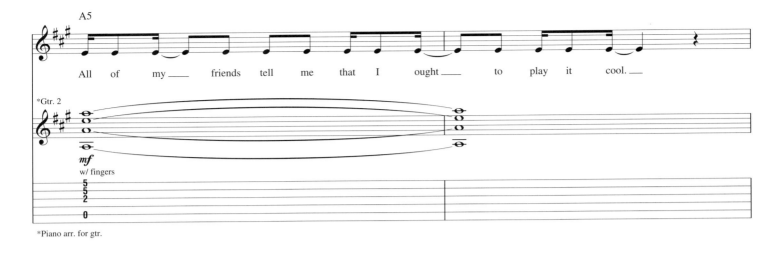
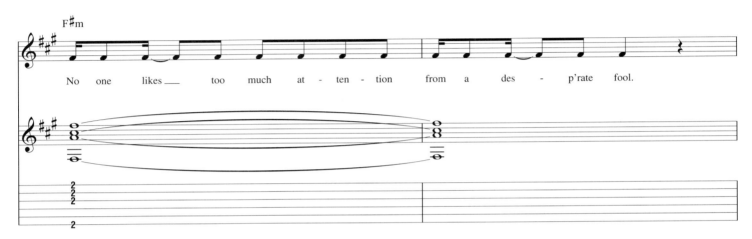

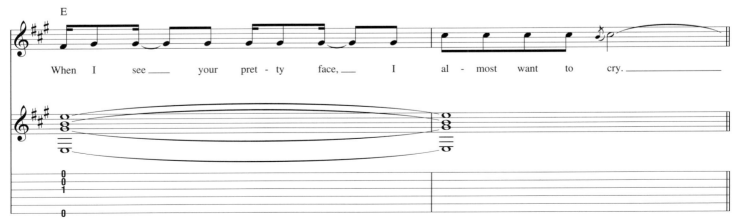

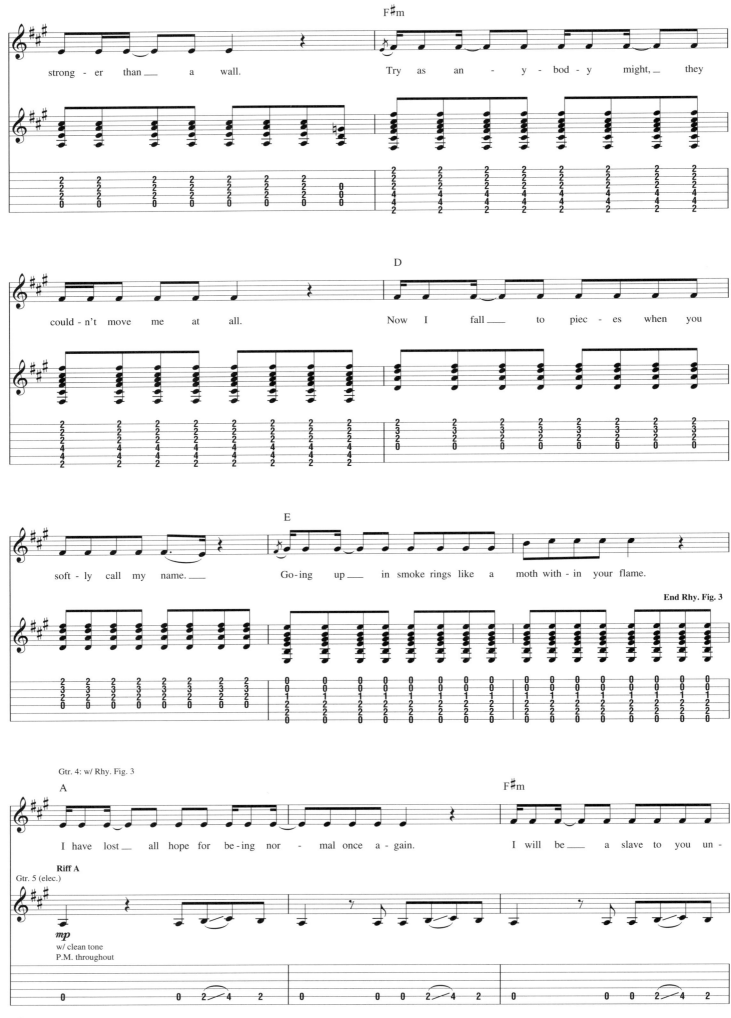

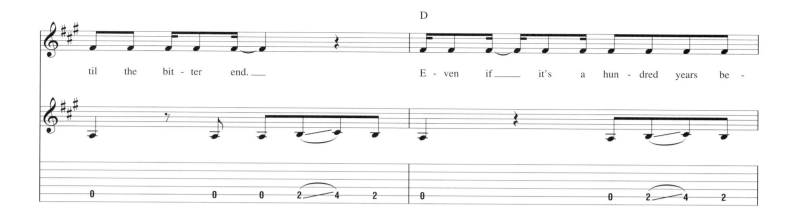

Chorus
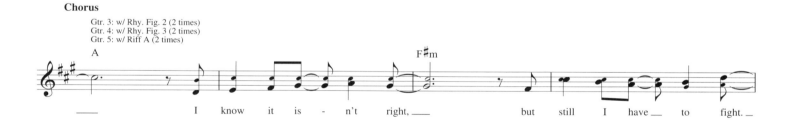
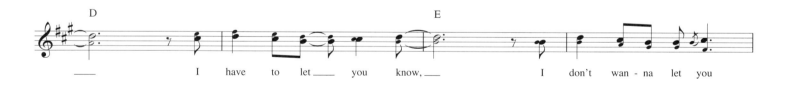
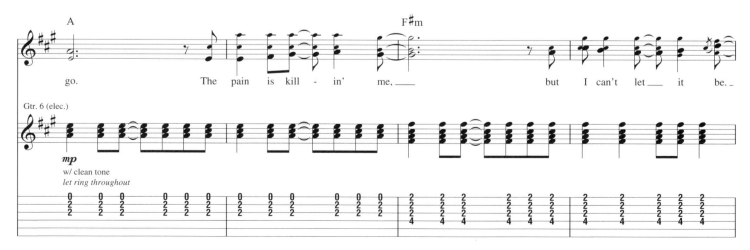

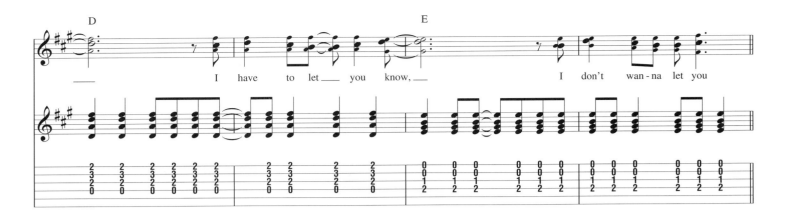
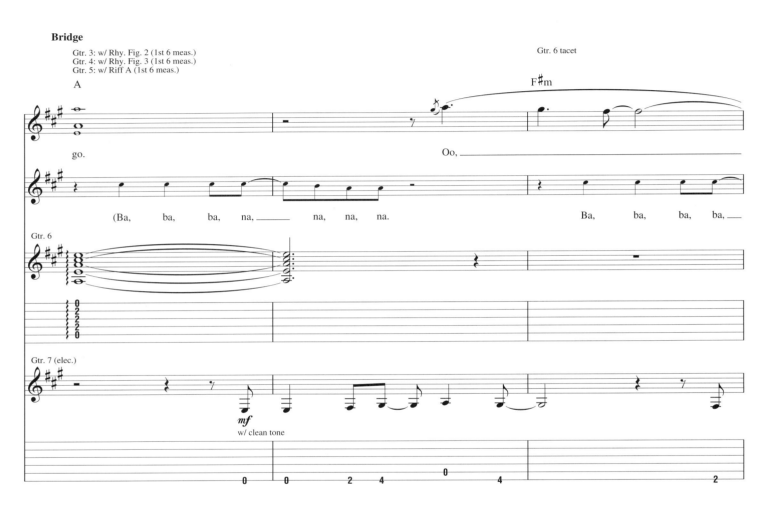
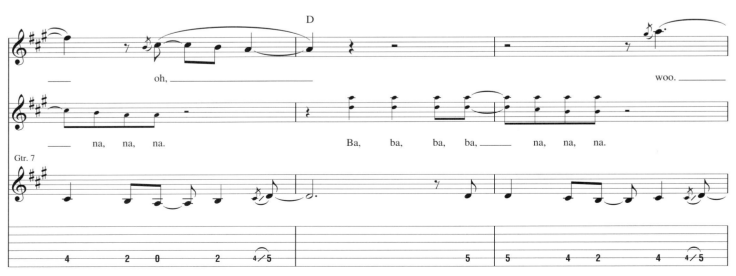

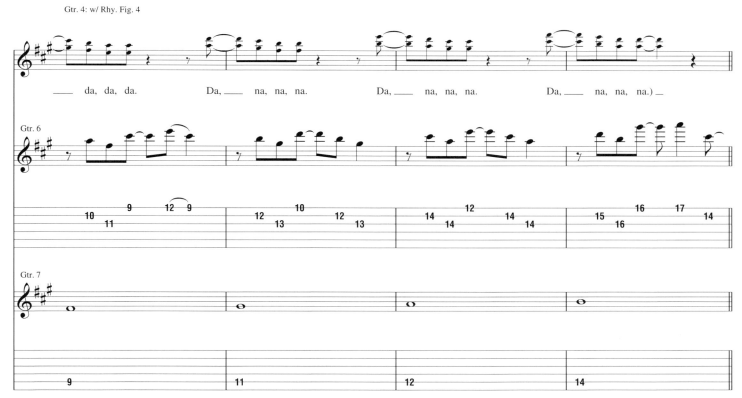

75

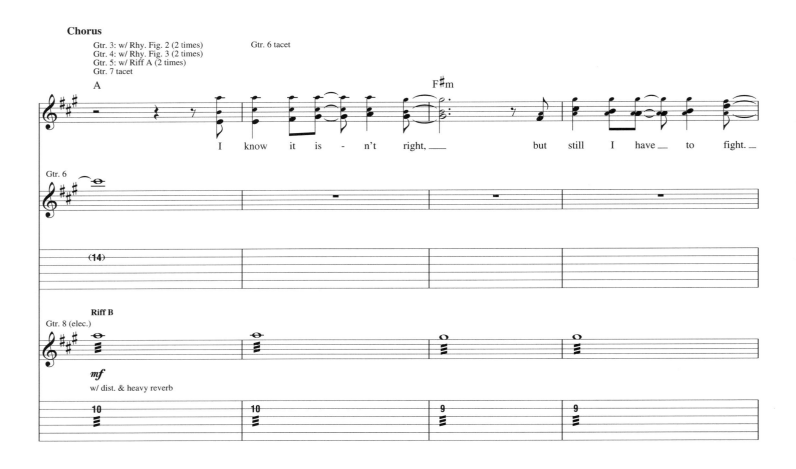
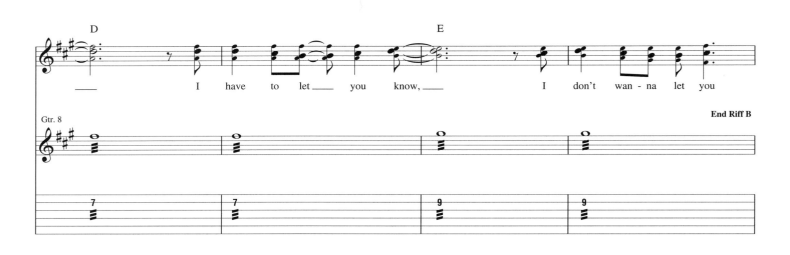
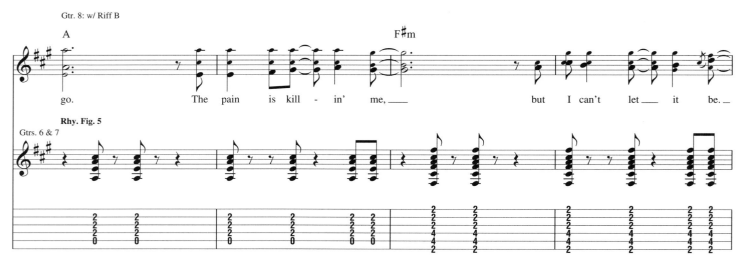

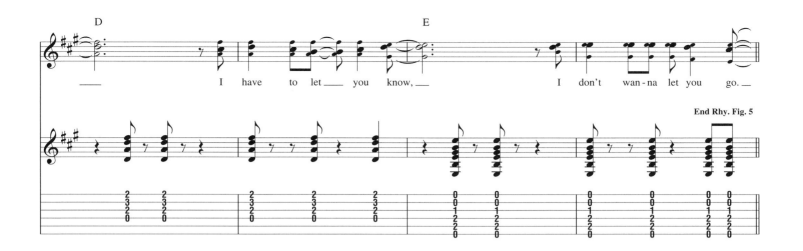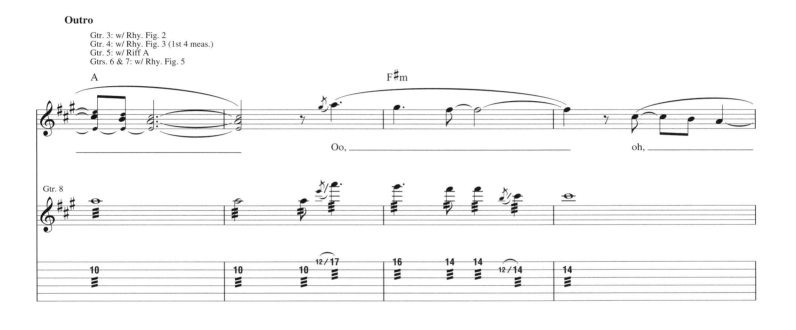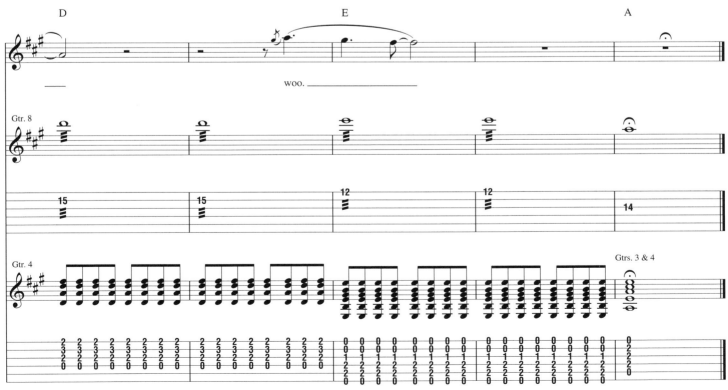

GUITAR NOTATION LEGEND

Guitar music can be notated three different ways: on a *musical staff*, in *tablature*, and in *rhythm slashes*.

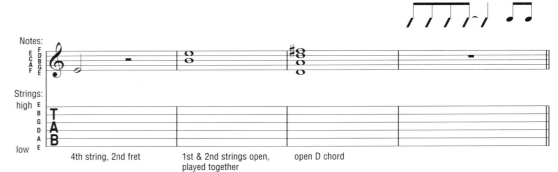

RHYTHM SLASHES are written above the staff. Strum chords in the rhythm indicated. Use the chord diagrams found at the top of the first page of the transcription for the appropriate chord voicings. Round noteheads indicate single notes.

THE MUSICAL STAFF shows pitches and rhythms and is divided by bar lines into measures. Pitches are named after the first seven letters of the alphabet.

TABLATURE graphically represents the guitar fingerboard. Each horizontal line represents a string, and each number represents a fret.

HALF-STEP BEND: Strike the note and bend up 1/2 step.

WHOLE-STEP BEND: Strike the note and bend up one step.

GRACE NOTE BEND: Strike the note and immediately bend up as indicated.

SLIGHT (MICROTONE) BEND: Strike the note and bend up 1/4 step.

BEND AND RELEASE: Strike the note and bend up as indicated, then release back to the original note. Only the first note is struck.

PRE-BEND: Bend the note as indicated, then strike it.

VIBRATO: The string is vibrated by rapidly bending and releasing the note with the fretting hand.

WIDE VIBRATO: The pitch is varied to a greater degree by vibrating with the fretting hand.

HAMMER-ON: Strike the first (lower) note with one finger, then sound the higher note (on the same string) with another finger by fretting it without picking.

PULL-OFF: Place both fingers on the notes to be sounded. Strike the first note and without picking, pull the finger off to sound the second (lower) note.

LEGATO SLIDE: Strike the first note and then slide the same fret-hand finger up or down to the second note. The second note is not struck.

SHIFT SLIDE: Same as legato slide, except the second note is struck.

TRILL: Very rapidly alternate between the notes indicated by continuously hammering on and pulling off.

TAPPING: Hammer ("tap") the fret indicated with the pick-hand index or middle finger and pull off to the note fretted by the fret hand.

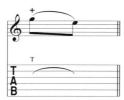

NATURAL HARMONIC: Strike the note while the fret-hand lightly touches the string directly over the fret indicated.

PINCH HARMONIC: The note is fretted normally and a harmonic is produced by adding the edge of the thumb or the tip of the index finger of the pick hand to the normal pick attack.

PICK SCRAPE: The edge of the pick is rubbed down (or up) the string, producing a scratchy sound.

MUFFLED STRINGS: A percussive sound is produced by laying the fret hand across the string(s) without depressing, and striking them with the pick hand.

PALM MUTING: The note is partially muted by the pick hand lightly touching the string(s) just before the bridge.

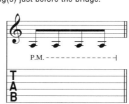

RAKE: Drag the pick across the strings indicated with a single motion.

TREMOLO PICKING: The note is picked as rapidly and continuously as possible.

VIBRATO BAR DIVE AND RETURN: The pitch of the note or chord is dropped a specified number of steps (in rhythm), then returned to the original pitch.

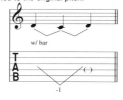

VIBRATO BAR SCOOP: Depress the bar just before striking the note, then quickly release the bar.

VIBRATO BAR DIP: Strike the note and then immediately drop a specified number of steps, then release back to the original pitch.

RECORDED VERSIONS®

The Best Note-For-Note Transcriptions Available

ALL BOOKS INCLUDE TABLATURE

00692015	Aerosmith – Greatest Hits	$22.95
00690178	Alice in Chains – Acoustic	$19.95
00694865	Alice in Chains – Dirt	$19.95
00690812	All American Rejects – Move Along	$19.95
00690958	Duane Allman Guitar Anthology	$24.99
00694932	Allman Brothers Band – Volume 1	$24.95
00694933	Allman Brothers Band – Volume 2	$24.95
00694934	Allman Brothers Band – Volume 3	$24.95
00690865	Atreyu – A Deathgrip on Yesterday	$19.95
00690609	Audioslave	$19.95
00690820	Avenged Sevenfold – City of Evil	$24.95
00690366	Bad Company – Original Anthology	$19.95
00690503	Beach Boys – Very Best of	$19.95
00690489	Beatles – 1	$24.99
00694832	Beatles – For Acoustic Guitar	$22.99
00691014	Beatles Rock Band	$34.99
00690110	Beatles – White Album (Book 1)	$19.95
00692385	Chuck Berry	$19.95
00690835	Billy Talent	$19.95
00690901	Best of Black Sabbath	$19.95
00690831	blink-182 – Greatest Hits	$19.95
00690913	Boston	$19.95
00690932	Boston – Don't Look Back	$19.99
00690491	David Bowie – Best of	$19.95
00690873	Breaking Benjamin – Phobia	$19.95
00690451	Jeff Buckley – Collection	$24.95
00690957	Bullet for My Valentine – Scream Aim Fire	$19.95
00691004	Chickenfoot	$22.99
00690590	Eric Clapton – Anthology	$29.95
00690415	Clapton Chronicles – Best of Eric Clapton	$18.95
00690936	Eric Clapton – Complete Clapton	$29.99
00690074	Eric Clapton – The Cream of Clapton	$24.95
00694869	Eric Clapton – Unplugged	$22.95
00690162	The Clash – Best of	$19.95
00690828	Coheed & Cambria – Good Apollo I'm Burning Star, IV, Vol. 1: From Fear Through the Eyes of Madness	$19.95
00690593	Coldplay – A Rush of Blood to the Head	$19.95
00690962	Coldplay – Viva La Vida	$19.95
00690819	Creedence Clearwater Revival – Best of	$22.95
00690648	The Very Best of Jim Croce	$19.95
00690613	Crosby, Stills & Nash – Best of	$22.95
00690967	Death Cab for Cutie – Narrow Stairs	$22.99
00690289	Deep Purple – Best of	$17.95
00690784	Def Leppard – Best of	$19.95
00692240	Bo Diddley	$19.99
00690347	The Doors – Anthology	$22.95
00690348	The Doors – Essential Guitar Collection	$16.95
00690810	Fall Out Boy – From Under the Cork Tree	$19.95
00690664	Fleetwood Mac – Best of	$19.95
00690870	Flyleaf	$19.95
00690931	Foo Fighters – Echoes, Silence, Patience & Grace	$19.95
00690808	Foo Fighters – In Your Honor	$19.95
00690805	Robben Ford – Best of	$19.95
00694920	Free – Best of	$19.95
00690848	Godsmack – IV	$19.95
00690601	Good Charlotte – The Young and the Hopeless	$19.95
00690943	The Goo Goo Dolls – Greatest Hits Volume 1: The Singles	$22.95
00694854	Buddy Guy – Damn Right, I've Got the Blues	$19.95
00690840	Ben Harper – Both Sides of the Gun	$19.95
00694798	George Harrison – Anthology	$19.95
00690841	Scott Henderson – Blues Guitar Collection	$19.95
00692930	Jimi Hendrix – Are You Experienced?	$24.95
00692931	Jimi Hendrix – Axis: Bold As Love	$22.95
00692932	Jimi Hendrix – Electric Ladyland	$24.95
00690017	Jimi Hendrix – Live at Woodstock	$24.95
00690602	Jimi Hendrix – Smash Hits	$24.99
00690793	John Lee Hooker Anthology	$24.99
00690692	Billy Idol – Very Best of	$19.95
00690688	Incubus – A Crow Left of the Murder	$19.95
00690544	Incubus – Morningview	$19.95
00690790	Iron Maiden Anthology	$24.99
00690721	Jet – Get Born	$19.95
00690684	Jethro Tull – Aqualung	$19.95
00690959	John5 – Requiem	$22.95
00690814	John5 – Songs for Sanity	$19.95
00690751	John5 – Vertigo	$19.95
00690845	Eric Johnson – Bloom	$19.95
00690846	Jack Johnson and Friends – Sing-A-Longs and Lullabies for the Film Curious George	$19.95
00690271	Robert Johnson – New Transcriptions	$24.95
00699131	Janis Joplin – Best of	$19.95
00690427	Judas Priest – Best of	$22.99
00690742	The Killers – Hot Fuss	$19.95
00690975	Kings of Leon – Only by the Night	$22.99
00694903	Kiss – Best of	$24.95
00690355	Kiss – Destroyer	$16.95
00690930	Korn	$19.95
00690834	Lamb of God – Ashes of the Wake	$19.95
00690875	Lamb of God – Sacrament	$19.95
00690823	Ray LaMontagne – Trouble	$19.95
00690679	John Lennon – Guitar Collection	$19.95
00690781	Linkin Park – Hybrid Theory	$22.95
00690743	Los Lonely Boys	$19.95
00690720	Lostprophets – Start Something	$19.95
00690955	Lynyrd Skynyrd – All-Time Greatest Hits	$19.99
00694954	Lynyrd Skynyrd – New Best of	$19.95
00690754	Marilyn Manson – Lest We Forget	$19.95
00694956	Bob Marley– Legend	$19.95
00694945	Bob Marley– Songs of Freedom	$24.95
00690657	Maroon5 – Songs About Jane	$19.95
00120080	Don McLean – Songbook	$19.95
00694951	Megadeth – Rust in Peace	$22.95
00690951	Megadeth – United Abominations	$22.99
00690505	John Mellencamp – Guitar Collection	$19.95
00690646	Pat Metheny – One Quiet Night	$19.95
00690558	Pat Metheny – Trio: 99>00	$19.95
00690040	Steve Miller Band – Young Hearts	$19.95
00694883	Nirvana – Nevermind	$19.95
00690026	Nirvana – Unplugged in New York	$19.95
00690807	The Offspring – Greatest Hits	$19.95
00694847	Ozzy Osbourne – Best of	$22.95
00690399	Ozzy Osbourne – Ozzman Cometh	$19.95
00690933	Best of Brad Paisley	$22.95
00690995	Brad Paisley – Play: The Guitar Album	$24.99
00690866	Panic! At the Disco – A Fever You Can't Sweat Out	$19.95
00690938	Christopher Parkening – Duets & Concertos	$24.99
00694855	Pearl Jam – Ten	$19.95
00690439	A Perfect Circle – Mer De Noms	$19.95
00690499	Tom Petty – Definitive Guitar Collection	$19.95
00690428	Pink Floyd – Dark Side of the Moon	$19.95
00690789	Poison – Best of	$19.95
00693864	The Police – Best of	$19.95
00694975	Queen – Greatest Hits	$24.95
00690670	Queensryche – Very Best of	$19.95
00690878	The Raconteurs – Broken Boy Soldiers	$19.95
00694910	Rage Against the Machine	$19.95
00690055	Red Hot Chili Peppers – Blood Sugar Sex Magik	$19.95
00690584	Red Hot Chili Peppers – By the Way	$19.95
00690852	Red Hot Chili Peppers –Stadium Arcadium	$24.95
00690511	Django Reinhardt – Definitive Collection	$19.95
00690779	Relient K – MMHMM	$19.95
00690631	Rolling Stones – Guitar Anthology	$27.95
00694976	Rolling Stones – Some Girls	$22.95
00690264	The Rolling Stones – Tattoo You	$19.95
00690685	David Lee Roth – Eat 'Em and Smile	$19.95
00690942	David Lee Roth and the Songs of Van Halen	$19.95
00690031	Santana's Greatest Hits	$19.95
00690566	Scorpions – Best of	$22.95
00690604	Bob Seger – Guitar Collection	$19.95
00690803	Kenny Wayne Shepherd Band – Best of	$19.95
00690968	Shinedown – The Sound of Madness	$22.99
00690813	Slayer – Guitar Collection	$19.95
00690530	Slipknot – Iowa	$19.95
00690733	Slipknot – Vol. 3 (The Subliminal Verses)	$22.99
00120004	Steely Dan – Best of	$24.95
00694921	Steppenwolf – Best of	$22.95
00690655	Mike Stern – Best of	$19.95
00690877	Stone Sour – Come What(ever) May	$19.95
00690520	Styx Guitar Collection	$19.95
00120081	Sublime	$19.95
00120122	Sublime – 40oz. to Freedom	$19.95
00690929	Sum 41 – Underclass Hero	$19.95
00690767	Switchfoot – The Beautiful Letdown	$19.95
00690993	Taylor Swift – Fearless	$22.99
00690830	System of a Down – Hypnotize	$19.95
00690799	System of a Down – Mezmerize	$19.95
00690531	System of a Down – Toxicity	$19.95
00694824	James Taylor – Best of	$16.95
00690871	Three Days Grace – One-X	$19.95
00690737	3 Doors Down – The Better Life	$22.95
00690683	Robin Trower – Bridge of Sighs	$19.95
00699191	U2 – Best of: 1980-1990	$19.95
00690732	U2 – Best of: 1990-2000	$19.95
00660137	Steve Vai – Passion & Warfare	$24.95
00690116	Stevie Ray Vaughan – Guitar Collection	$24.95
00660058	Stevie Ray Vaughan – Lightnin' Blues 1983-1987	$24.95
00694835	Stevie Ray Vaughan – The Sky Is Crying	$22.95
00690015	Stevie Ray Vaughan – Texas Flood	$19.95
00690772	Velvet Revolver – Contraband	$22.95
00690071	Weezer (The Blue Album)	$19.95
00690966	Weezer – (Red Album)	$19.99
00690447	The Who – Best of	$24.95
00690916	The Best of Dwight Yoakam	$19.95
00690905	Neil Young – Rust Never Sleeps	$19.99
00690623	Frank Zappa – Over-Nite Sensation	$19.95
00690589	ZZ Top Guitar Anthology	$24.95

FOR A COMPLETE LIST OF GUITAR RECORDED VERSIONS TITLES, SEE YOUR LOCAL MUSIC DEALER, OR WRITE TO:

HAL•LEONARD® CORPORATION

7777 W. BLUEMOUND RD. P.O. BOX 13819 MILWAUKEE, WI 53213

Visit Hal Leonard online at **www.halleonard.com**

Prices and availability subject to change without notice. Some products may not be available outside the U.S.A.

0310

GUITAR *signature licks*

Signature Licks book/CD packs provide a step-by-step breakdown of "right from the record" riffs, licks, and solos so you can jam along with your favorite bands. They contain performance notes and an overview of each artist's or group's style, with note-for-note transcriptions in notes and tab. The CDs feature full-band demos at both normal and slow speeds.

ACOUSTIC CLASSICS
00695864 .... $19.95
AEROSMITH 1973-1979
00695106 .... $22.95
AEROSMITH 1979-1998
00695219 .... $22.95
BEST OF AGGRO-METAL
00695592 .... $19.95
DUANE ALLMAN
00696042 .... $22.95
BEST OF CHET ATKINS
00695752 .... $22.95
THE BEACH BOYS DEFINITIVE COLLECTION
00695683 .... $22.95
BEST OF THE BEATLES FOR ACOUSTIC GUITAR
00695453 .... $22.95
THE BEATLES BASS
00695283 .... $22.95
THE BEATLES FAVORITES
00695096 .... $24.95
THE BEATLES HITS
00695049 .... $24.95
BEST OF GEORGE BENSON
00695418 .... $22.95
BEST OF BLACK SABBATH
00695249 .... $22.95
BEST OF BLINK - 182
00695704 .... $22.95
BEST OF BLUES GUITAR
00695846 .... $19.95
BLUES GUITAR CLASSICS
00695177 .... $19.95
BLUES/ROCK GUITAR MASTERS
00695348 .... $21.95
KENNY BURRELL
00695830 .... $22.99
BEST OF CHARLIE CHRISTIAN
00695584 .... $22.95
BEST OF ERIC CLAPTON
00695038 .... $24.95
ERIC CLAPTON – THE BLUESMAN
00695040 .... $22.95
ERIC CLAPTON – FROM THE ALBUM UNPLUGGED
00695250 .... $24.95
BEST OF CREAM
00695251 .... $22.95
CREEDANCE CLEARWATER REVIVAL
00695924 .... $22.95
DEEP PURPLE – GREATEST HITS
00695625 .... $22.95
THE BEST OF DEF LEPPARD
00696516 .... $22.95

THE DOORS
00695373 .... $22.95
ESSENTIAL JAZZ GUITAR
00695875 .... $19.99
FAMOUS ROCK GUITAR SOLOS
00695590 .... $19.95
BEST OF FOO FIGHTERS
00695481 .... $24.95
ROBBEN FORD
00695903 .... $22.95
GREATEST GUITAR SOLOS OF ALL TIME
00695301 .... $19.95
BEST OF GRANT GREEN
00695747 .... $22.95
BEST OF GUNS N' ROSES
00695183 .... $24.95
THE BEST OF BUDDY GUY
00695186 .... $22.95
JIM HALL
00695848 .... $22.99
HARD ROCK SOLOS
00695591 .... $19.95
JIMI HENDRIX
00696560 .... $24.95
JIMI HENDRIX – VOLUME 2
00695835 .... $24.95
JOHN LEE HOOKER
00695894 .... $19.99
HOT COUNTRY GUITAR
00695580 .... $19.95
BEST OF JAZZ GUITAR
00695586 .... $24.95
ERIC JOHNSON
00699317 .... $24.95
ROBERT JOHNSON
00695264 .... $22.95
BARNEY KESSEL
00696009 .... $22.99
THE ESSENTIAL ALBERT KING
00695713 .... $22.95
B.B. KING – THE DEFINITIVE COLLECTION
00695635 .... $22.95
B.B. KING – MASTER BLUESMAN
00699923 .... $24.99
THE KINKS
00695553 .... $22.95
BEST OF KISS
00699413 .... $22.95
MARK KNOPFLER
00695178 .... $22.95
LYNYRD SKYNYRD
00695872 .... $24.95
BEST OF YNGWIE MALMSTEEN
00695669 .... $22.95

BEST OF PAT MARTINO
00695632 .... $24.99
WES MONTGOMERY
00695387 .... $24.95
BEST OF NIRVANA
00695483 .... $24.95
THE OFFSPRING
00695852 .... $24.95
VERY BEST OF OZZY OSBOURNE
00695431 .... $22.95
BEST OF JOE PASS
00695730 .... $22.95
TOM PETTY
00696021 .... $22.99
PINK FLOYD – EARLY CLASSICS
00695566 .... $22.95
THE POLICE
00695724 .... $22.95
THE GUITARS OF ELVIS
00696507 .... $22.95
BEST OF QUEEN
00695097 .... $24.95
BEST OF RAGE AGAINST THE MACHINE
00695480 .... $24.95
RED HOT CHILI PEPPERS
00695173 .... $22.95
RED HOT CHILI PEPPERS – GREATEST HITS
00695828 .... $24.95
BEST OF DJANGO REINHARDT
00695660 .... $24.95
BEST OF ROCK
00695884 .... $19.95
BEST OF ROCK 'N' ROLL GUITAR
00695559 .... $19.95
BEST OF ROCKABILLY GUITAR
00695785 .... $19.95
THE ROLLING STONES
00695079 .... $24.95
BEST OF DAVID LEE ROTH
00695843 .... $24.95
BEST OF JOE SATRIANI
00695216 $22.95
BEST OF SILVERCHAIR
00695488 .... $22.95
THE BEST OF SOUL GUITAR
00695703 .... $19.95

BEST OF SOUTHERN ROCK
00695560 .... $19.95
MIKE STERN
00695800 .... $24.99
ROD STEWART
00695663 .... $22.95
BEST OF SURF GUITAR
00695822 .... $19.95
BEST OF SYSTEM OF A DOWN
00695788 .... $22.95
ROCK BAND
00696063 .... $22.99
ROBIN TROWER
00695950 .... $22.95
STEVE VAI
00673247 .... $22.95
STEVE VAI – ALIEN LOVE SECRETS: THE NAKED VAMPS
00695223 .... $22.95
STEVE VAI – FIRE GARDEN: THE NAKED VAMPS
00695166 .... $22.95
STEVE VAI – THE ULTRA ZONE: NAKED VAMPS
00695684 .... $22.95
STEVIE RAY VAUGHAN – 2ND ED.
00699316 .... $24.95
THE GUITAR STYLE OF STEVIE RAY VAUGHAN
00695155 .... $24.95
BEST OF THE VENTURES
00695772 .... $19.95
THE WHO – 2ND ED.
00695561 .... $22.95
JOHNNY WINTER
00695951 .... $22.99
BEST OF ZZ TOP
00695738 .... $24.95

FOR MORE INFORMATION,
SEE YOUR LOCAL MUSIC DEALER,
OR WRITE TO:

HAL•LEONARD®
CORPORATION
7777 W. BLUEMOUND RD. P.O. BOX 13819
MILWAUKEE, WISCONSIN 53213

www.halleonard.com

COMPLETE DESCRIPTIONS AND SONGLISTS ONLINE!
Prices, contents and availability subject to change without notice.

0410